MANAGING LEADERSHIP PARADOXES

Managers today are faced with numerous complex challenges speckled with paradoxes. They must have a sharp economical focus while simultaneously engaging in creative and innovative thinking. They must support individuals as well as teams, think globally, and do business locally. This book views complexity as a fundamental element of leadership, rather than something that should simply be reduced and removed. It presents a leadership concept that includes both sides of the paradox.

Managing Leadership Paradoxes uses case studies and practical exercises to show how managers can maintain decisiveness in the face of paradoxes, complexities, and contradictory demands. Lotte Lüscher draws on research gleaned from managers within the international corporation, Lego, to provide first-hand knowledge of how a large-scale organization meets and manages change paradoxes, rather than treating them as something that needs to be reduced and removed. It will assist managers and aspiring managers in expanding their understanding of leadership challenges beyond dilemmas, and equip them with the managerial skills to handle the most persistent and pervasive paradoxical challenges that arise as a result of organizational change.

The book will be of interest to leaders and managers, as well as students of leadership, management, and organizational studies. The intent is to provide the reader with a foundation for reflecting on his or her own leadership practice with special focus on organizational complexity, ambiguity, and paradoxes.

Lotte S. Lüscher, Founder, Clavis Business Psychology, and external lecturer, Aarhus Business School and the Department of Psychology, Aarhus University, Denmark.

"Lotte Lüscher inspires leaders to not only work through but to thrive with paradoxes - the interwoven contradictions that pervade our organizations and our leadership lives. Through insights and examples she demonstrates the value of engaging tensions, accepting paradoxical challenges as opportunities for innovation and improvement. Such a paradox mindset holds promise for more sustainable approaches to leading in times of rising change, ambiguity, and competing demands."

Marianne W. Lewis, *Dean and Professor of Management, Cass Business School, City University, London*

"Leadership is full of paradoxes and every leader struggles to cope with them. This book digs into the heart of what paradox is and how to deal with the dilemmas that confront us every day. Everyone with leadership aspirations should read it."

Morgen Witzel, *Fellow, Exeter Centre for Leadership, UK*

"Leading does not have a definite answer. No 5-step recipe or a handful of tools will solve it for you. This book leads you to a paradoxical mindset to face paradoxical organizational life. A must-read for leaders who want to develop their mindset for facing the paradoxes of organizations and still be able to lead."

Wendy Smith, *Professor, University of Delaware, USA*

MANAGING LEADERSHIP PARADOXES

Lotte S. Lüscher

LONDON AND NEW YORK

First published 2019
by Routledge
2 Park Square, Milton Park, Abingdon, Oxon OX14 4RN

and by Routledge
711 Third Avenue, New York, NY 10017

Routledge is an imprint of the Taylor & Francis Group, an informa business

© 2019 Lotte S. Lüscher

The right of Lotte S. Lüscher to be identified as author of this work has been asserted by her in accordance with sections 77 and 78 of the Copyright, Designs and Patents Act 1988.

All rights reserved. No part of this book may be reprinted or reproduced or utilised in any form or by any electronic, mechanical, or other means, now known or hereafter invented, including photocopying and recording, or in any information storage or retrieval system, without permission in writing from the publishers.

Trademark notice: Product or corporate names may be trademarks or registered trademarks, and are used only for identification and explanation without intent to infringe.

British Library Cataloguing-in-Publication Data
A catalogue record for this book is available from the British Library

Library of Congress Cataloging-in-Publication Data
Names: Lüscher, Lotte S., author.
Title: Managing leadership paradoxes / Lotte S. Lüscher.
Description: 1 Edition. | New York : Routledge, 2019. | Includes bibliographical references and index.
Identifiers: LCCN 2018015592 | ISBN 9781138497047 (hbk) | ISBN 9781138497054 (pbk) | ISBN 9781351019941 (ebk)
Subjects: LCSH: Leadership. | Organizational change. | Teams in the workplace–Management.
Classification: LCC HD57.7 .L867 2019 | DDC 658.4/092–dc23
LC record available at https://lccn.loc.gov/2018015592

ISBN: 978-1-138-49704-7 (hbk)
ISBN: 978-1-138-49705-4 (pbk)
ISBN: 978-1-351-01994-1 (ebk)

Typeset in Bembo
by Out of House Publishing

Printed and bound by CPI Group (UK) Ltd, Croydon, CR0 4YY

CONTENTS

List of figures and tables	*viii*
Author biography	*ix*
Preface	*xi*
Acknowledgments	*xiv*

PART I
Paradoxical leadership as a way of thinking   1

1	Complex leadership	3
	Goals of this book	4
	The paradox: a mental construction	8
	Layout of this book	9
2	A leadership concept across paradigms	13
	Leadership on the paradigm bridge	14
	What is leadership?	15
	The modern leadership paradigm	16
	The postmodern leadership paradigm	17
	On the bridge: leadership between paradigms	24
	Chapter summary	25
3	The Lego project: an encounter with leadership's paradoxes	26
	Narrative about an action research project	26
	Lego's 11 leadership paradoxes	28
	Managerial issues	29

Brainstorming: conversation toward paradox 31
Summary 43

PART II
Paradoxical leadership development 45

4 The organizational paradox: the paradox inherent in
  organizational life 47
  Organizational paradoxes at Lego 47
  Communication: the system's contradictions 50
  A tool for strategic-change projects: Competing Values Framework 53
  Summary 59

5 Organizational paradoxes in practice: examples of
  organizational change 61
  Carletti: organizational strengths and managerial needs 61
  Status of the organization with CVF as a tool 62
  Strategic development initiatives 63
  Summary 67

6 The role paradox: contradictory demands of leadership 68
  Role paradoxes in Lego 69
  CVF and personal leadership 72
  Manager roles between change and stability 72
  Leadership roles between results and relationships 80
  Summary 89

7 Role paradoxes in practice: examples of leadership
  development 91
  Role paradoxes: toward clarity regarding tasks and roles
    within the management team 91
  Role paradoxes: toward mutual understanding within the
    management team 96
  Summary 98

8 Paradox of belonging: the emotional aspect 100
  Lego's paradoxes of belonging 101
  The tool: dialogue about ambivalence 104
  The Stockdale paradox 107
  Workable certainty through the paradox of belonging 108
  Leadership in paradoxes of belonging 109
  Summary 111

9	The paradoxes of belonging in practice: moving toward relationships and a well-functioning management team	113
	The paradox of belonging: trust–control	113
	The autonomy paradox	117
	The paradox of belonging: propriety–honesty	118
	Summary	119

PART III
Leading through paradox: acceptance, positioning, and integrative thinking 121

10	Integrative thinking	123
	Leading through integrative thinking	125
	Vision Tech	125
	Summary	130
11	Reflective distance, oscillation, and positioning	132
	Personal tendencies and preferences within paradoxes	133
	The paradox exercise	134
	The pitfalls	136
	Fear	137
	Reflective distance	137
	Positioning theory	140
	Summary	144
12	Acceptance	146
	Acceptance: a paradoxical solution	150
	Creating acceptance within the organization	151
	Summary	152
13	Managerial flow: leading through paradox	154
	Paradoxes are interwoven	155
	Paradoxes: a leadership mindset	157
	Leadership concepts of the future: do they include paradoxes?	159
	Conclusion	161

Bibliography	*163*
Index	*167*

FIGURES AND TABLES

Figures

3.1	The sense-making model	32
4.1	Competing Values Framework: organizational paradoxes	54
4.2	Competing paradigms	58
5.1	Focus on the external polarities of the paradoxes	63
5.2	Movement toward the internal poles in the paradox	66
6.1	The wheel of leadership roles	73
7.1	Current role focus of a leadership team: Karsten	93
7.2	Current role focus of a leadership team: Lisbeth	94
7.3	Current role focus of a leadership team: Hanne	94
11.1	The paradox exercise: the positive opposite	136
11.2	The paradox exercise: too much of the opposite	138
11.3	Meeting forums where you can work with leadership of strategy and operation	139
11.4	Exploration of contradictory positions within the paradox	142
12.1	Mutual sense-making, manager–employee relationship	148
13.1	The connection between paradoxes	155

Tables

2.1	The modern versus the postmodern leadership paradigms	21
2.2	The modern versus the postmodern manager	25
4.1	Organizational paradoxes	52
6.1	Role paradoxes	71
8.1	Paradoxes of belonging	102
11.1	The paradox exercise	135
11.2	The paradox exercise: prominent leadership qualities	135

AUTHOR BIOGRAPHY

Lotte S. Lüscher holds an MSc in psychology and a PhD in business psychology from Aarhus Business School. She is the founder of Clavis Business Psychology, an external lecturer at Aarhus University, a leadership consultant, and the author of various books about leadership. She works primarily as a leadership consultant for Danish companies with focus on leaders and leadership teams. Lotte also teaches paradox leadership at the University of Aarhus on executive educational programs and MBAs. As a consultant, she is especially interested in the way in which managers must navigate complexity and ambiguity within organizations. Her book, *Leading Through Paradox* (2012), has been translated and published in English and her latest book has been published in Danish: *The Leader Between Doubt and Action* (2018).

PREFACE

I was inspired to write this book after working with an investigative project at Social and Business Sciences at Aarhus University entitled "Working Through Paradox." I was enthusiastic about the new and exciting results of the project. Throughout my education, as well as my work as a manager and consultant, I had encountered various theories and models that could be used in order to understand good management. I found that these theories focused on thinking about *either* strategic *or* personal management. I also often encountered the term organizational management, but I never fully understood the meaning of this concept, aside from the fact that it had to do with matching various organizational forms to corresponding tasks in the workplace. I found myself searching for an approach that would last – an understanding of management that could guide me in my work as a consultant and partner with organizations seeking to develop their management practices. However, many of the management theories I encountered were one-dimensional, and I found them to be constantly trying to "one-up" earlier theories, which were actually just as valid as the theory trying to replace them.

Thanks to the opportunity to work with managers and directors within Lego's supply chain, as well as dialogue with management in various businesses and public institutions, I have experienced the possibilities of working with a management approach that includes complexity, conflicting demands, and ambivalence. I have also found that this complexity can provide an advantageous basic understanding of management tasks, rather than being an obstacle that must be reduced and eliminated.

For example, I discovered that management can reduce complexity and confusion through implementing clear rules, procedures, and a stable workflow. However, focusing on this reduction will in turn create a need for flexibility, new thinking, creativity, and exploration within the organization. Any solution will generate a new problem. Conversely, the organization will become a stressful environment and lose a sense of direction if management constantly focuses on new thinking, conversion, innovation, and vision. A management theory needs to include both ends of the spectrum, as well as all the management tools that are necessary to implement such an approach.

It is important to note that the use of a management theory is, in itself, a way of reducing complexity. The use of a management theory creates a frame of shared language and understanding with which to comprehend one's organizational reality. Like many other management theories, paradox-management simply offers a framework for thinking about management. Thinking in terms of the paradoxes between renewal and stability, or well-being and effectiveness, still creates a model which is unable to describe the complexity and multifaceted problems that we meet in our ever-changing surroundings. The model reduces management into dichotomies, and it can be argued that the world is too complex to allow for simply thinking in ambiguities. As a student recently suggested to me, should we not instead think in "multi-doxes" in order to include additional dimensions of leadership and the inherent complexities this requires?

I have chosen to focus on dichotomies, because at the moment my brain cannot accommodate additional dimensions. The work I have done to expand organizational problems in order to find non-reductive understandings of all the "either-or," "both-and" dilemmas, difficult managerial choices, and treatment of managerial actions is a big enough mouthful for now. Even though the requirements of management today discourage accommodating further complexities, I propose that the solution to organizational problems lies first and foremost in the challenge of including the contradictory, ambivalent and ambiguous, while still maintaining managerial drive. As a manager I worked with, recently said:

> I am good at creating structure and avoiding ambiguity by providing a framework, direction, and clarity regarding resources and space for each of my managers. They know what they have to work with. I have done turnarounds in many organizations, but it seems as if people don't follow along with my thinking after a while. I end up creating so much clarity that the managers stop questioning me – it is as if all that clarity has a reverse side. They jump when I say jump, and don't come down again until I tell them to – and that is not what I need if we are going to develop our organization. But you can't be good at everything– or can you?

Managing Leadership Paradoxes sets out to accommodate the reverse side of any management initiative. As a manager, it is important to know that while there is a need to turn your attention in a certain direction, there is a simultaneous need to watch that which you are turning away from, so that you can respond to it if it becomes relevant again.

This book is addressed to managers who are searching for a deeper understanding of the defining elements of the management discipline. What is the role of management, and how can a manager navigate within complex and contradictory organizations? This book offers not only tools and leadership technologies, but also a basic understanding of management as a discipline where one-time solutions do not exist.

It is my hope that, by reading this book, you experience the same epiphany that I found at the end of my long journey in order to define good leadership. However, you will not find a simple answer to that question here. Instead you will find a management concept that can accommodate the inherent complexity of the management discipline.

If you feel that you have read many books, participated in numerous management courses, and gained several management tools, yet still lack answers about how your management style creates action and clarity in your organization, then this book is for you. My hope is that after reading this book, you will be able to share your understanding with your organization so that together you can create a management style where complexity and paradoxes are a part of your daily work experience.

The most important themes in this book are:

- The opportunities and limitations of the predominant management paradigms, as well as some information about how they guide/limit our management options.
- Paradox as an opportunity for committed leadership.
- Examples of three types of paradoxes which you can relate to your management practice.
- Tools for developing strategy within the management team, as well as tools for implementing these strategies in order to develop management.
- Thinking in paradoxes as a basis for complex solutions to complex problems.
- A discussion of how all this complexity and understanding of paradoxes leads you forward as a manager.

ACKNOWLEDGMENTS

I have received a lot of help in writing this book. Camilla Duus and Lars Dalby Gundersen from Clavis Business Psychology and Kuno Johansen from Gellert-Johansen have tirelessly supported me, contributed to the practical development of the book, and kept me on track in writing about all of the deeply meaningful examples of reflective leadership that we meet throughout our consultant work. I would especially like to recognize Camilla and Kuno for their efforts in reading the book and providing comments and feedback.

Peter H. Thomsen from Keylearning has also helped me through his contributions to the development of the quadrant-model and reflective conversations. In addition, Thomas Raunsbaek from Raunsbaek Consulting ApS has been an invaluable partner in the development of our company and leadership test MPI, "Management of Paradox Indicator," which has been a useful tool for working with management development. I must also thank Anne Staerk who has contributed many relevant reflections throughout the writing of our combined article, "Leading in postmodern times." Thanks to Andreas Juhl for allowing me to work with a management development project where paradoxes became visible and extremely relevant to practical work.

Thanks as well to the Danish Academy of Defence, Michael Rose, and Kristian Malver, who allowed me to use their management model FOKUS as inspiration to rethink the Competing Values Framework Model.

Finally, a thank you to all the companies that have shared their complex issues with me, let me work as a process consultant and learner and talked with me in consultancy sessions. Together with you I have also learned to accept everything that remains unseen, paradoxical, and ultimately – inspiring...

PART I
Paradoxical leadership as a way of thinking

1
COMPLEX LEADERSHIP

Managers today are faced with a number of complex challenges: They must have a sharp economical focus while simultaneously engaging in creative and innovative thinking. They must support individuals as well as teams, think globally, and do business locally. They must have focus on people and relationships, as well as focusing on achieving results. The list goes on and on. Within the management role we can identify a number of paradoxes which result from the demand for managers to successfully negotiate complex issues.

Several years ago I spent three years as the manager of a project organization. During that time I was constantly searching for an understanding of what good leadership entailed. I wanted to become a good leader. However, I felt that if I involved my employees too much in the decision-making process, my leadership wasn't visible enough. On the other hand, if I tried to be firm and visible through decisions and clear directives, I found that my employees didn't feel seen or acknowledged. In addition, I attempted to focus on building relationships with my employees because I knew that people are motivated by good cooperation, good social relations, and a strong team. However, this resulted in the board of directors demanding that I was able to cut through and require more of my employees. I felt trapped between a focus on relationships and a focus on results.

After those three years as a manager, I had the opportunity to implement an action research project with a group of managers from Lego and the Business School at Aarhus University, Denmark. During the project I had a double role as both actor and researcher, due to the fact that I was working as both consultant and researcher. This meant that I used information from the processes I was a part of in order to study the development that I – or we – had initiated.

I found that many of the Lego managers described the same types of problems I had experienced myself. They felt as if they were caught between ambiguous demands and conflicting tasks. They found that it was difficult to provide direction while still maintaining clarity regarding their roles as leaders. I was reminded of my own experiences throughout my time as a manager, as well as the times I had seen several managers grapple with their own leadership development. These paradoxes were often confusing, and created a feeling of paralysis. As a result of these observations, I was curious to discover how leadership could be understood with its complexities and ambiguity intact. This book is therefore addressed to managers who would like to learn how they can navigate the many conflicting demands of their organization.

Goals of this book

This book has two goals:

1. To present an understanding of leadership that is simple and understandable while still including complexity, ambiguity, and paradox.
2. To show that the concept of paradoxical leadership can be used as a practical way of thinking in order to create managerial drive in complex and ambiguous situations. This will allow managers to periodically evaluate and make the appropriate managerial adjustments in order to meet the organization's goals and strategies.

It is easy to identify the paradoxes within an organization, but it is much more difficult to discover how leaders should act *within* these paradoxes. This chapter will present you with a way of thinking about management tasks paradoxically. The chapter introduces an understanding of leadership as a discipline that maintains all of its complexities. I will start by briefly summarizing how leadership has been understood throughout recent history. I will then advocate for an integration of the various historical understandings of what a leader should focus on in order to obtain success in his or her organization. We will see how leadership should consist of old-fashioned, traditional management virtues as well as newer, more equal understandings of the manager–employee relationship. This combination is essential in order for management to become an effective tool and fulfill the goals of the organization. Newer forms of leadership have naturally arisen from, among other things, research pointing to the fact that employees who are involved in decisions and feel valued by management are more motivated and therefore work better. However, at the same time, I often hear employees requesting clearer guidelines and greater transparency regarding the organization's direction. This results in a situation where the manager must provide a clear direction and take on an autocratic position.

This book will not profess a preference for one or the other type of leadership, nor will it accept that managers will do what they always have done according to their personality or personal preference. Instead, I hope to demonstrate that managers can benefit from a leadership approach which contains opportunities for periodic reflection and adjustment of managerial effort in regard to the organization's leadership needs. This book is not intended as yet another "how to do" guide (there are many of those!) but more as a "how to think" guide. In other words, this book allows you to reflect upon your leadership practices in a way that combines the organizational complexity with the ambiguities and paradoxes you meet throughout the leadership discipline.

There are many strategies and corporate management theories that have arisen from long-dead theorists and organizational "engineers" who introduced principles for organization, leadership and growth in the previous century. These very traditional principles continue to form the way in which companies distribute resources, create budgets, distribute power, reward employees, make decisions, etc. Their goal has been (and still is) to create stability, predictability, and clarity through guidelines, direction, purpose, and goals.

In response to this traditional approach, rising attention has been placed on concepts such as complexity, ambiguity, "multi-verses," internal consistency, contrasts, and paradox. These concepts are most often used in research regarding organizational changes, leadership, and innovation/creativity. For example, some researchers point to the fact that the act of creating an organization raises questions about simultaneous demands regarding centralizing vs. involvement, collective vs. individual, stability vs. change, streamlining vs. complexity, and preserving an organization's core identity vs. innovation. In other words, we no longer see organizations as stable entities that must manage a changing environment, but instead as renewable, dynamic systems that contain the seeds of change. More and more we see organizations as fluctuating processes, rather than as stable structures with fixed procedures and completely coordinated behavior. Organizations are currently perceived as a set of activities which coordinate our understandings and create a shared mental structure that grounds us in a world of changing uncertainty. As a result, traditional leadership tools become more and more difficult to use when situations change. Managers need to be able to act within the organization in different ways in accordance with different times and changing challenges. Tools to create structure, stability, and clarity fall short of this challenge.

Today there is recognition of the fact that companies that want to survive must be equipped to handle constant changes in products, organization, marketing, etc. However, despite this recognition, we often see that change is understood (both in practice and in leadership literature) as deep, radical turnarounds, where everything must be re-thought from the beginning. This raises the question of how equipped an organization actually is if it ends up replacing directors, implementing radical re-structuring, rethinking products, etc. In this model, single individuals are considered as having "hero-status." The idea is, "we'll replace the director and somewhere find the person that can implement exactly the type of change we want." This is a common tendency in European companies, where turnarounds (a new director with fundamentally different ideas) demonstrate that change is still primarily understood as a top-down process with closely planned missions, events, goals, and actions.

The limitation of this model is that when the director is replaced, the entire basis for the organization's existence must be re-discovered by the next director. It can be beneficial to replace a director, but it is also a costly and lengthy process to find and orient a new director. Therefore, it might be more effective to have a director (or manager or other management position) who can operate with the company's diverse needs over time. Leadership is managing complexity. This does not mean reducing complexity, but rather helping employees to operate *within* complexity.

In today's world, management groups must be able to create organizations that can continually renew themselves and switch focus between operation and renewal. In the book, *The Future of Management* (2010), Hamel uses the body as an analogy for the ability for ongoing adaptation. I will use the following examples to illustrate his point: When the body is exposed to new physical challenges the heart pumps faster, which in turn provides the muscles with more blood. When you stand in front of an audience to give a presentation, your adrenaline levels rise in order to sharpen your performance. When you see someone you are attracted to, your pupils automatically contract. Hamel claims that challenges faced by organizations are the same as those faced by the body, even though this is not a usual method used to describe organizations. Like the body, organizations must develop automatic, responsive, adaptive systems that can be changed and renewed continually, spontaneously, and without crisis.

Within organizational change there are many disciplines that are worth considering when a company needs to handle the challenge of coping with ongoing change. Strategic thinking, economics, decision-making, budgeting, logistics, structure, marketing strategies, accounting, and leadership psychology must be incorporated in a non-traditional manner. For example, many companies still find that the process of creating a reward structure that promotes team performance without compromising individual performance is a great mystery. According to Hamel, all management courses should be thrown up in the air and fundamentally re-thought in order to create context and task-dependent courses. This would allow managers to meet leadership challenges while focusing on what they want to achieve according to various times and various organizational challenges.

I hope that this book will establish a leadership concept that can help managers navigate the ground between renewal and stability, as well as between a focus on relationships and on bottom lines as forms of leadership change in accordance with changing demands and focus. I hope to create an understanding of leadership as a compass, leadership that can create renewal and maintain continuity, leadership that involves employees, and leadership that first and foremost is about following the organization's need instead of following personal strengths and preferences.

Leadership: Toward "Workable certainty." Workable certainty can be defined as situations where total certainty is not possible, due to contradictory and ambiguous demands, but where there remains just enough certainty for work to take place. There is a significant amount of management literature which claims that handling the changes, diversity, and variation in an organization calls for leaders who can show the way, create clarity, and find "workable certainty" for the employees.

March and Olsen (1976) describe organizations as "meaning-creation" entities which use communication and symbolic interaction as procedures for argumentation and interpretation. They claim that organizational life is based on a negotiated and shared understanding of reality. This shared understanding lays the foundation for organizational decisions and actions.

A manager's task is to create meaning between opposing pieces of information, to select relevant information, and share the selected information with the goal of creating what Karl Weick (1995) calls "workable certainty." Certainty is an illusion, but organizational actors are always engaged in the process of creating meaning through their own understanding and interpretation of the flow of information. Our actions are created by our own understandings, not by an objective reality. This model of understanding organizational life is called a social-constructionist approach, because it builds upon the way in which we create our reality through communication and shared understandings.

The social-constructionist perspective of leadership uses language in order to create shared meaning and direction in organizations. We continually negotiate, coordinate, hold meetings, clarify tasks, inform others, and create more or less shared meaning because we have a need for perceiving reality as ordered, fixed, and understandable. Concepts such as "shared meaning" and "workable certainty" are considered objective realities, not constructed concepts. For example, at the time this book was written, Denmark was going through an "economic crisis." Formulating the crisis as objective reality means that we must contemplate a long list of logical actions. We believe that the crisis means it is dangerous to spend money, and therefore think, "I should probably wait to buy a house," or management groups decide to wait to hire a human resources employee. Business clients are also wary of investing in long-term investments, since an economic crisis often means that it is better to focus on the short term. The fact that we have a shared concept called "economic crisis" makes us react in accordance with all of the "performances" that are attached to the concept of crisis. This results in the idea of an economic crisis being maintained as a shared reality.

Of course we each ask ourselves what we must do when we are in a crisis situation. Naturally, the answer is to be frugal, create plans for saving, and develop strategies for growth. In Chinese, the word "crisis" is translated into two words, which together mean "threat" and "opportunity." *Politiken Business Erhvervssider* (October 28, 2009) states,

> The word "crisis" didn't exist in traditional China. There was a word/symbol for "danger," and a word for "opportunity." Therefore, when modern China needed to create a word for "crisis," it was decided to combine the two symbols. The result of this combination is that crisis (*weiji*) causes alarm-bells to ring, but in an energizing way. There is danger, but the danger creates opportunities if the situation is handled correctly. Crisis does not have the same paralyzing effect in Asia as it does in the West. Instead it is a phenomenon that requires action.

There is a huge difference between talking about a crisis using "threat language" (barriers and frugality as a sounding-board) and talking about crisis using "opportunity language" (where innovative thinking and adaptation are welcomed). Here is one example:

There is currently an interesting concept of "the welfare gap" that is discussed during management education and conferences. This concept shows that there is a marked gap between the welfare demands of the future and the economic and human resources that are currently available. The question is, should we see "the welfare gap" as a burning platform, or as an opportunity for much-needed innovative thinking in the generation of welfare services?

There are volumes of information and communication that create a shared working reality within organizations. Our shared working reality is created through meetings and dialogue, as well as in the cafeteria and all the places where we talk about our organization. The task of management is to secure a clear direction and "workable certainty" for the employees. Management needs to make sense from the ambiguous demands on individuals and the management team. At the same time, they must use that sense in order to help the members of the organization make sense collectively, which moves them toward "workable certainty."

The paradox: a mental construction

One of the challenges that arises in complex arenas is to use paradox as the basis for decision-making. Paradox can be defined in the following way: A paradox arises when two true and mutually exclusive elements (thoughts, feelings, or actions) show themselves to be interconnected when seen in relation to one another.

How can something be mutually exclusive and yet interconnected? For example, many companies are currently experiencing the reality that they must reduce costs *and* expand, as well as maintaining the working status quo *and* implementing renewal. This can be seen in the public sector where institutions must improve performance *and* cut down on performance. These situations are often experienced as contradictions, but they could also be seen as interconnected elements. Paradox arises when these elements of thought/statement/emotion/action are brought together and we realize that both elements are true and can, in fact, be managed with the same solution.

The recognition of paradox can be experienced as paralyzing. It isn't immediately apparent how one should handle a paradox. An example of a paradox could be that a manager must listen to employees in order to ensure that they feel seen, heard, and understood, while at the same time a manager must be able to be efficient and establish direction. A leader that I had a conversation with formulated the problem like this:

> I sit there with the employee-satisfaction survey and realize that the employees want me to listen more, become more involving. The last time we did the

survey they said that I needed to be more effective and visible in meetings. So I can't figure out whether I should turn left or right anymore…

Although it isn't always clear how to act in a paradox, it is also impossible to simply remain within the paradoxical situation. This causes paralysis and difficulty finding a course of action. In the previous example, the manager cannot simply sit back and allow the employees to manage themselves while simultaneously being visible and providing directives. Paralysis occurs when we experience two or more competing "orders" or incentives that pull us in opposite directions. We often call this a dilemma because it feels as if we must make a decision that will cost us something either way. This is paralyzing because we can't choose one element without losing the other, and we therefore feel that we can't succeed no matter what we choose to do. If we see this in connection with the demand to create workable certainty, we can see that managers must relate to paradoxes in order to "unparadoxize." The only possible way to manage this complex situation is to create a new understanding that includes both ends of the paradox, but also points toward adequate actions. Paradoxes are, in other words, paradoxical: You can't act within a paradox, but you can't escape it either!

The paradoxical perspective builds on the assumption that humans are inherently good at operating within an ambiguous, contradictory world with many conflicting truths. The assumption is that we are good at navigating this complicated world in order to create meaning, a sense of direction, and the ability to act. However, as a consultant, I often find that there is a great need to delimit, "uncomplicate," and create meaning out of the many ambiguous demands that are placed on organizations and managers today.

Therefore, throughout this book we will work with the question of how to find paths to lead us toward workable certainty when we encounter paradox. It is crucial for a manager's success that he or she can manage paradox and accept that it is impossible to avoid. At the same time, it is a manager's task to create the drive to act within an organization.

My hope is that managers, and future managers, will be able to recognize the paradoxical perspective of leadership that is explained in the book, and that this will allow managers to accommodate the complexity involved in leadership. Although this book has a broad understanding of leadership, the point is that good leadership starts with managers relating to paradox and living with the fact that paradox cannot be eliminated. My hope is that managers and management teams can use this book in order to form an overview of some of the contradictory and paradoxical issues that arise in connection with creating meaning, direction, and scope in a complex and changing organization.

Layout of this book

This book consists of three sections:

Part I is the theoretical section. Here leadership is understood within the frame of paradoxes. In this introductory chapter I have introduced the need to develop a leadership concept that matches organizational complexity. I have described leadership as a complex phenomenon that contains a number of dilemmas, ambiguities, and ambivalence. I have also identified the need for thinking about leadership from a paradoxical perspective which accommodates complexity and ambiguity, as well as contradictory demands within the manager role.

In Chapter 2 we will explore the leadership concept and discuss leadership as a socially constructed phenomenon. Early leadership concepts (lead, distribute, and control) will be contrasted with what can be called postmodern leadership concepts (consultative and motivating functions). I will argue that in order to maintain an understanding of leadership in organizations, we must reintroduce some of the old leadership virtues while simultaneously discussing leadership in the relational coaching terms of newer literature. Leadership needs to include both aspects of setting limits and providing motivation.

In Chapter 3 I describe the Lego project that led me to the concept of leading through paradox. The chapter introduces concrete examples of how paradox is relevant for organizational transformation. Among other things, I describe a case study with Lego which created the starting point for an investigative project about leadership undergoing transformation. Lego has included paradoxical thinking as a part of its foundation for management several times. The latest of these was in connection with the investigative project, "Working through Paradox," which I completed in collaboration with the company in 2002. During the project I had the opportunity to investigate three types of paradox. These paradoxes have also been the focus of other investigators who are interested in leadership and transformation. The three levels, or types, of paradoxes that managers can relate to are: Organizational paradox, role paradox, and the paradox of belonging. Toyota is used as an example of a company that has successfully navigated these central paradoxes.

In Part II you can see how you can work with paradox as a tool in different situations. These situations include when you and your management group must analyze organizational status (Chapters 4 and 5), determine concrete leadership behavior that matches leadership needs, be sure that communication is clear, and work as simply as possible with paradox as an element of team-work.

Chapter 4 presents a model for the understanding of some of the issues that companies must balance. We explore and explain organizational paradoxes between stability and change, and between results and relations. In this chapter I was especially inspired by Quinn and Cameron's concept of competitive values, the Competing Values Framework Model.

Chapter 5 builds on Chapter 4 and illustrates how some leadership groups have worked with organizational paradoxes in practice in order to create change in strategic focus.

Chapter 6 describes role paradoxes and provides examples of some of the leadership positions that reflect organizational paradoxes. I describe leadership behavior, not based on personal qualities or strengths, but instead founded on a relational starting point. This starting point is based on the answer to the question "How can I, as a manager, best position myself in order to support the organization's need for leadership at the moment?" I will use Lego as an example in order to show how their managers attempted to create meaning using concrete paradoxical leadership challenges.

Chapter 7 explains MPI (Management of Paradox Indicator) as a tool for leadership development. I provide an example of how a management group uses MPI in order to create a new understanding of their role paradoxes as well as an evaluation of their own leadership roles/positions. The exercise can also be used by groups of managers who want to develop together, find out how they can pay attention to relevant organizational challenges, and how they can adjust their leadership efforts to match the needs of their organization.

Chapter 8 introduces the most difficult paradox to work with: the paradox of belonging. This paradox deals with the emotional aspects of organizational life and the ambivalence that causes us to act and communicate with employees in ambiguous, contradictory and confusing ways.

Chapter 9 provides options for how a leadership group can work to confront paradoxes of belonging as well as challenging themselves and each other to live with and communicate about ambivalence as part of organizational life.

Part III describes ways of navigating and balancing paradox. Three ways of relating to paradox are introduced: integrative thinking, positioning, and acceptance.

Chapter 10 examines integrative thinking as a way that managers can use paradox constructively. For example, in decision-making, managers must complete a simultaneously analytic and creative process that eliminates paradox to such a point where leadership is possible and the will to act is maintained. Examples of this decision-making process are strategic and central decisions that affect the company or leadership efforts.

Chapter 11 introduces another way of relating to paradox: positioning. Positioning refers to keeping paradoxical alternatives separate by handling them separately. This can be done by recognizing that although there are times when you have to ignore one part of the paradox, it still continues to exist as a demand. For example, if you show faith in your employees and turn your back on focusing on control, you still have to be aware of the need to make sure that everything runs smoothly. Different types of focus are required at different times. This is an approach to paradox that is especially connected to leadership roles. I use some examples of positioning as well as some concrete tools in order to reflect on which positions are helpful when dealing with concrete leadership paradoxes.

Chapter 12 examines acceptance as another, more fundamental approach to paradox. In complex companies that operate with complex issues, managers will always be required to create meaning and workable certainty from leadership paradoxes. Paradoxes are a mental construction, and thinking in paradoxes requires a paradoxical acceptance of complex contradictory and ambiguous tasks that are a part of a changing organization.

Chapter 13 summarizes paradoxical thinking as fundamental approach to leadership and provides perspective in relation to using paradox for strategic decisions, in leadership focus areas, and in relation to communication within the organization. The manager's task is to communicate clearly and concisely about ambiguous subjects as well as to set a direction where flexibility and the unknown are a part of daily life. Overall, their task is to operate with and understand that paradox and complexity are part of leadership, while simultaneously clarifying paradoxes and creating workable certainty for employees.

I hope that managers who are eager to navigate complexity and ambiguous demands on leadership have developed an appetite to read further. The next chapter provides a foundation for understanding paradoxical leadership as a leadership concept that crosses the boundaries of classic and new leadership theories.

Before moving on to Chapter 2, I would like to include a brief explanation about the use of the terms manager, management, leader, and leadership in this book. These terms will be used interchangeably throughout the book. This is due to the fact that the book was originally written in Danish, and the Danish terms "leder" and "ledelse" do not distinguish between leadership and management. In addition, the organizational structure of Danish companies is relatively non-hierarchical, and the difference between managerial positions is not as significant as it can be in other cultures. Therefore, I would encourage you to read and think about the concepts in this book using the terms you find most appropriate to your role and organization.

2
A LEADERSHIP CONCEPT ACROSS PARADIGMS

In the previous chapter I described two main characteristics of leadership theory. The first described leadership characteristics of guidance, visibility, and boundary-setting. The other described the leadership characteristics of developing employee potential, empathy, listening, and support.

These approaches, or points of view, are also called paradigms. A paradigm is a set of assumptions that contains all the theories that adhere to a particular point of view.

In this chapter two paradigms are contrasted:

1. The "modern" paradigm is built on the assumption that there is *one* truth for the good, true, and correct way to organize. Within the modern paradigm we find leadership theories that focus on forms of leadership that are visible, provide guidance, and define frameworks.
2. The "postmodern" paradigm is based on the idea that good leadership is negotiated and created through interactions. Therefore, within the postmodern paradigm there are assumptions about the fact that equality and dialogue are the way forward in creating a shared reality for both managers and employees. This paradigm suggests leadership theories that focus on involving, supportive, and communicative forms of leadership.

How can we simultaneously understand these apparently contradictory leadership paradigms?

Theoretically, they contradict each other. But can they be connected? And how can we think about leadership as a discipline that contains both ways of thinking and builds a bridge between the paradigms?

Paradoxical leadership means that you as a leader must stand on the bridge between these paradigms and combine them in order to ensure a flexible set of leadership decisions.

Leadership on the paradigm bridge

In 2008 I published an article together with Anne Staerk in the periodical *Business Psychology* (*Erhvervspsykologisk*) with the title "Leadership in the post-modern perspective: is it possible?" ("Ledelse I det postmoderne – hvordan gør man det?") The article was an attempt to build a bridge between paradigms. This section refers to this article, where we argue for a new introduction of "old" leadership virtues.

In today's organizations, employees are expected to be more independent than ever before, while simultaneously being expected to be team-oriented. Managers are expected to delegate, while simultaneously expected to control. Independent teams, courses in self-management, and leadership courses on coaching and employee motivation are more popular than ever. This points to the fact that today's employees must be prepared to be highly self-propelled in everything they do. Concepts such as commitment, empowerment, teamwork, delegation, etc. are all about strengthening employees' competences for self-management and autonomy.

The more controlling aspects of the leadership role include leadership surveys, satisfaction surveys, time registrations, and employee interviews. These elements direct and limit the behavior of employees. Through these elements it is possible for management to ensure that employees fall within a set of expectations.

This picture reveals a number of paradoxical demands of the current manager role. Managers must both be efficient *and* responsive, and they must take the lead *and* recede into the background. The paradoxical demands of leadership arise from the managerial context that exists today. Complex demands of organizational innovation, rapid change and agility on one side, and reliable deliveries, stable and firm market positions, and solid production on the other create a context for leadership, where newer leadership paradigms (innovation leadership, self-managing employees, team development) supplement, but don't replace, traditional leadership paradigms (control, measurement, job descriptions, etc.) (e.g. Alvesson & Sveningsson, 2003).

As a consultant, I often experience that satisfaction surveys are common in companies where managers received criticism, either because they aren't responsive enough or because they are not visible enough and don't provide directives. If managers involve employees in visions and goals, they risk having employees feel that they lack guidelines and direction. However, if the managers provide guidelines and direction, they risk having employees feel that they are not heard and don't have ownership of the organization's direction. Therefore, the question is whether managers should dictate what happens, or whether they should involve employees in decision-making, despite the danger that they might choose a different direction.

> An administrative director in a large production company expressed his expectation that middle-management would take initiative and risks in order to increase development and create a larger sense of leadership for each manager. After much hesitation, the managers began to take initiative and make independent decisions. However, the director felt that these decisions did not mesh with the overall direction that he and the Board of Directors

had chosen. Should the director now go in and stop the initiatives that the sales-department had launched? Or should he first and foremost praise the initiative and independent decisions? As he said, "I can't ask them to be independent and then, when they comply, say that independence is to do the same thing that I would have done, can I?"

In the example above, many directors would go in and stop the initiatives in order to live up to the board of directors' expectations. However, this would have a huge cost in the form of neglected feelings of responsibility and ownership within the manager group. The paradox is that the director must create independent individuals who do what is expected…

In leadership literature, these demands are reflected within various leadership paradigms which partly consist of defining and directing activity, and partly of involving and coaching activity. In the article, "Leadership in the post-modern perspective" (Lüscher & Staerk, 2008), we called these two types of leadership paradigms postmodern and modern in accordance with the assumptions that form the way leadership is understood.

Therefore, a central question is: how can leaders understand their roles in a context where they must both provide guidelines and directives/directions to their employees, and yet simultaneously create dialogue and emotional involvement? In my practice as a leadership consultant, I can see how the paradigms live side by side within companies, as well as a large degree of lack of clarity regarding the roles of leadership.

What is leadership?

Leadership is often defined across various theories as a process where leadership exercises influence on others in order to achieve organizational goals. In other words, leadership occurs when a person has influence over a group of individuals in order to achieve a shared goal. But what does it mean to exercise influence? When seen through a social-constructionist perspective, influence involves structuring the potential field of action of others through explanations that provide meaning for employees (Shotter, 1993).

In the definition above, the linguistic element of the leadership task is emphasized. Communication is central, in the form of information, dialogue, and explanations. Although linguistic communication is an essential condition for discussing leadership, I will allow myself to broaden the definition to include a variety of other activities such as designing the physical space, distribution of resources, and organization of work tasks. These activities are not direct linguistic actions, but they are essential for the optimal success of employee's tasks. Therefore, my definition of the leadership purpose is:

> The purpose of leadership is to create meaningful frameworks so that employees can succeed in their tasks as efficiently as possible, and thus contribute to the realization of organizational goals.

What assumptions about leadership lie behind this definition? There is a leadership ideal and a theory about the relationship between a leader and employees behind every leadership concept. Although there are many versions and degrees of leadership concepts, I will compare the modern and social-constructionist leadership concepts in order to investigate how the paradigms that steer our understanding of leadership contain a number of contradictions. As a consequence of these contradictions, there are many paradoxical demands made on the leaders of today's organizations.

The modern leadership paradigm

The modern (which herein includes the traditional) leadership perspective is based on the idea that there is *one* truth about the best way to run a company. When leadership has found this truth, the task is then to become a personified example of this truth, act as a role model for employees, and therefore inspire them to perform the "best practice." The idea of best practice is reflected in, among other things, praise and criticism as central leadership concepts. The function of these concepts is to correct employees and help them to find *the* correct way. The assumption behind this approach to leadership is that there is an objective right or wrong way to lead.

The leadership ideal in this paradigm is the *directing manager*, where the manager is the one who makes decisions and provides clear rules that employees must follow. This can be understood as "the superior's duty is to formulate the subordinate's duty" (Andersen & Born, 2001, p. 80). This idea is valid both in relation to specific work-tasks and in relation to the company's overall goal. Here the manager's task is to instill the company goal into the employees.

Since the manager's directives are central in this leadership paradigm, an essential leadership task is to control and supervise employees in order to ensure that the directives are followed. This is an external form of control. It is the manager who takes on the position of control, and from that position he or she attempts to discipline the employees in order to optimize effort within the organization. Therefore, the manager–employee relationship is characterized as *asymmetrical* in the modern leadership paradigm. This is a point that researchers such as Kirkeby (2001) emphasized in their understanding of the manager concept. The manager exercises his or her influence through educating, mastering, steering, and/or leading the employees. This is done from a position that is clearly asymmetric with the employee. The manager must encourage the employee to fit within the guidelines of the company, and the employee is paid to do so. There is a rational exchange of services and payment.

Another essential leadership concept of the modern leadership paradigm, aside from praise/criticism and various concrete reward systems, is various personality tests. In these personality tests, employees are categorized into almost diagnostic boxes which "show who they are." The manager can use this categorization to, for example, give the "correct" employees specific tasks, and create the "correct" work constellations.

However, there are a number of limitations involved in committing leadership to one paradigm. The majority of managers don't do this, but allow me to give an example that illustrates the limitations anyway:

> I had a conversation with a director who worked for a large contract manufacturer. He was in charge of a course of action that needed to follow a clear strategy. The idea was that the employees would take ownership of the strategy, so that it wouldn't end up being a "drawer-strategy." In our conversation, the director explained that he had needed to create a strict time registration in order to ensure that each employee's time was spent on the appropriate task. There had been too much wasted time, and the goal was to get a little more work for their money. Therefore, time registration and time-cards were implemented so that it could be seen who was taking breaks, where, and for how long. Rules were also made for how long a break could be, and what occasioned a break. The director told me that he had forbidden salespersonnel to have private conversations of any sort on company telephones. "And then I went on a business trip," he said, "and sure enough, there were people who cheated on their time-cards and placed international phone calls. No one would admit it was them, but it says something about how much you only think about yourself and how important it is to establish fixed rules."

In this example we can see how a leadership approach can reinforce itself if a manager does not question the validity of a controlling approach. The manager–employee relationship is relevant here. We can see that a lack of ownership was answered with even more control, which again led to less ownership, and so on.

The power relationship between a manager and employees can be understood by what White (2004) (using Foucault's words) calls *traditional power*. Traditional power is external power. It is something that is held and used by specific individuals (in this situation, managers) in relation to specific interests. The manager can use this power to limit, forbid, impose, etc. in relation to employees, and the employees are subject to the manager's power.

The postmodern leadership paradigm

At the end of the 1980s the so-called "newer" leadership paradigm appeared as a consequence of practical demands on organizations and philosophical concepts of what we call the postmodern age. There was resistance to the idea that there was only *one* objective truth and best practice in leadership literature. Instead, the idea was raised that there were many localized truths and corresponding best practices. The truth, and what was correct and desirable, was now understood as localized truths which were constructed through shared linguistic and "co-creative" practices.

As a consequence of this way of thinking, leadership is understood in a more consultative light. This is due to the fact that the manager in the postmodern perspective cannot instruct and direct *the* truth about what employees should do, nor in what direction employees should develop, because *the* truth does not exist. In other words, the manager cannot transfer his or her truth directly to the employee since truth is constructed through social and linguistic relationships.

As a result, the role of the manager has been changed dramatically. Employees are connected to their workplace in a completely different way than through the rational exchange. Instead of having a relationship of exchange, where the employee provides work and receives a paycheck, the employee is expected to demonstrate "commitment" which can be exchanged for engagement. Commitment builds upon the assumption of volunteerism, as well as an idea that if employees' attachment is strengthened through high levels of engagement and ownership, they will be more effective and do more for the organization. Andersen & Born (2001, in Lüscher & Staerk, 2008, p. 26) point out that the fundamental demand on the employee today is "a passion for work and the organization." The goal is no longer that of the modern leadership paradigm, where rational exchange dominates. Instead, the goal is that employees are emotionally attached to the organization. Essential leadership tools therefore become the involvement of employees' emotions, moods, and attitudes toward the job.

This leadership style is more personally involved, and it implies that employees must be involved in the organization on a deeper level than was common in the modern leadership paradigm. Employees must be prominently involved in work with vision, values, and strategy in order for them to feel ownership for their work. Rather than setting demands or providing rules and directions, the manager must now delegate responsibility and competence while supporting and motivating the employees. Instruction and distribution of tasks are no longer the central leadership tasks. They have been replaced by employee involvement through the delegation of responsibility and competences.

In a coaching session with a department manager in a company, we worked with how she could speed an employee up and help him to succeed with the things she has asked him to do multiple times. The manager identified that the organization had hired academic employees, and that it was therefore important for the employees to have a high degree of autonomy and freedom for organizing their work. They did not appreciate being controlled or being told how they should work. But now she had this employee who time after time had been told that he should develop a new product. Each time that the manager asked about the product the employee said that he was too busy. The manager had also had a conversation with the employee about how he could pass on some of his other assignments, and therefore have more time to complete the new product development, since he was the only one who could do it. The employee had said that that was fine, and that he would try to finish it as soon as he could. However, the manager was still unsatisfied because she knew that often nothing came of these conversations and she was beginning to be irritated. However, at the same time, she felt caught in her own assumptions about what was motivating for the employee:

> We have not had a culture where you rush people. They are well-educated, independent, and talented people, so I can't sit and control them and make

demands. We have an assumption that employees will organize things themselves. However, I do feel that he should be able to do more, but I also don't know about his work area, so I don't actually know how I can get him to do it. I'm also not a tough, old-fashioned manager. That's not the style here.

The manager in this example is mostly focusing on postmodern leadership virtues, which is smart in relation to the organization and culture of the company. However, at the same time she experiences that this focus falls short. It is impossible to lead completely through emotional engagement and personal ownership if the dialogue is worn out and the employee still has the last word about his work.

The changing relationship between manager and employee means that managers can no longer make decisions in the same way they did earlier, and they must therefore occupy a more equal position with their employees. The power gap between managers and employees, especially in the Scandinavian countries, has become narrower and narrower in recent years, which also indicates that managers are becoming more equal to their employees. The relationship between the manager and the employee is therefore becoming symmetric rather than asymmetric. Some of the forums that are established in organizations indicate that postmodern leadership forms have resulted in a displacement of power toward more equal relationships. For example, many companies use satisfaction surveys and APV (Danish abbreviation for workplace evaluation), where employees have the opportunity to evaluate management and share whether they are satisfied with the management they are "subjected to."

In the postmodern period there is also an increasing individualization of work, which means that the individual employee has the opportunity to create, and trust, individual agreements about development and self-realization with his or her manager. This is emphasized through, among other things, a particular type of conversation, known as the employee development interview (MUS). This type of conversation is described as a "lively" and "mutual" dialogue between employees and their immediate manager, with the purpose of providing the best possible opportunity for the employees to develop and flourish. This allows the employees to receive feedback on their work, but the intention is that the same forum should be used to provide the manager with feedback, in order to ensure that the employees are as satisfied as possible with the way that management is conducted. It is essential that the employees have responsibility for managing their own competence development. In other words, it is important that they are not told what areas need improvement, what courses they should take, etc., but instead discover this on their own.

As we can see in the section above, the forms of contact between managers and employees are moving toward more dialogue-based relationships. Essential management forums are participatory meetings, employee development interviews, or vision/value/strategy seminars. This paradigm is also reflected in leadership-based coaching sessions, where the manager coaches employees through a question which is intended to increase consciousness, feelings of responsibility, and employee commitment. Feedback no longer consists of praise and criticism, but of recognition and appreciation. This type of feedback is termed as a non-judgmental form of communication, where the employee is seen, heard, and understood, but not evaluated and judged. In the postmodern forms of leadership, the manager does not sit above the employees, but rather sits alongside them and attempts to understand their perspective while simultaneously encouraging the employees to "unfold" their own ideas, wishes, and aspirations.

Several years ago, a book called *Leadership-based Coaching* (Ledelsesbaseret coaching) was published (Soeholm et al., 2006). It provides some instructions for how managers can use their leadership position for coaching, but it also identifies the limitations of the coaching method. It points out that managers are still first and foremost leaders, which created a different relationship to the employee than the one that is typically experienced in a more equal coaching session.

The postmodern form of leadership operates with a different power relationship: that of a symmetric, rather than asymmetric relationship between manager and employee. This form of power, which Foucault called the *modern power*, can be understood as the ability to define meaning and is, despite the name, related to the postmodern way of thinking. This is an indirect form of power, which the manager does not exercise over employees, but which instead is exercised through the expectations that are implicit within the leadership forms of the postmodern paradigm. The fact that the power is indirect means that employees are expected to be self-reliant and manage framework, guidelines, and scope themselves. However, they are still expected to act along the lines of "what is expected." However, in the end, it is management that evaluates whether an employee's use of power is satisfactory, and therefore management still has the ultimate power. You could say that indirect power is built on the fact that employees are raised to demonstrate ownership and connection to the demands of the organization. Foucault identifies that this allows for the possibility for manipulative power, in that it is no longer good enough to do what you're told, but you must really *want* to do it yourself. Through emotionally connecting employees to the organization and management, managers and organizations can hope that employees acquire the norms and visions of the organization. If this happens, there will be a convergence between the vision, goals, and targets of the organization and the employees. Modern power is difficult to make visible, because it appeals to the individual's "obvious" engagement in the organization. Therefore, it occasionally falls short in situations where the connection is not so obvious after all.

Modern power is difficult to eliminate, because it is seen as voluntary. Modern power often shows itself in the fact that individuals have high work-ethics and own ideas about how and how much to give to the company, etc. However, because of this, it connects itself to a notion that the manager–employee relationship is equal.

Table 2.1 shows that juxtaposition between the newer leadership paradigm (postmodern leadership paradigm) and the traditional paradigms (modern leadership paradigm).

TABLE 2.1 The modern versus the postmodern leadership paradigms

	Modern	*Postmodern*
Basic assumptions	Realism/Functionalism	Relativism/Social-constructionist
	Universal truths	Local, subjective truths
Leadership ideal	Managers as directors	Managers as consultants
Leadership tools	Asymmetry	Symmetry
	Managers as experts	Manager among equals
	Rational exchange	Emotional exchange
Power relationships	Traditional power (external power, where someone has power over others)	Modern power (norm power, where power is internalized in the individual as norms, engagement, etc.)

Source: Inspired by Lüscher & Staerk (2008).

The idea of pursuing symmetry and eliminating power in a manager–employee relationship initially seems paradoxical. Is it possible to lead in a symmetrical relationship? Or is the leadership concept stuck between two poles, where on the one side we identify someone to create frameworks and results for employees, while on the other side we describe leadership from the premise that only motivated, self-leading employees complete their tasks?

Most of the definitions of leadership describe leadership as using influence, as we described at the beginning of the chapter (Northhouse, 1997). You could say that managers are attributed more power than the employees they lead. That it is, in fact, essential that the manager should have more power in the organization than the employees. If we assume that leadership basically is about someone having formal and official power in order to influence the good (and less good) ways to achieve organizational goals, then we are talking about traditional leadership.

Managers have the right to define and set normative frameworks for work. Based on this idea, concepts such as coaching, empathy, and emotional commitment are sufficient as leadership tools. However, despite the fact that social-constructionist tools are beneficial in practice, there is a need for managers to exert influence through providing frameworks and being both more directive and more normative.

If we do not recognize the traditional power relationship as an essential part of the leadership concept, but instead use only a modern power relationship, we find ourselves in a situation where managers need to "sneak" leadership into the workplace. In other words, they have to sneak around in order to steer the organization in the desired direction. An example of this can be found in the following excerpt of a conversation with an employee:

> So I know that when my manager comes to me and says, "Claus, you would probably be good at this task, is it something you would be interested in? The customer is asking for you and I think that it is juuust the right task for you!" that it is because he doesn't want to give me an order. And sometimes it can be a really tiresome job, that neither I nor others in the organization want, but when it is served to me, packed up in acknowledging and motivational terms, then you don't want to say no, right? I know that "No" is not really an option, my manager has just learned that it isn't motivating to get an order. But I think it would be a more honest and clearer way to manage.
>
> *From a conversation in 2006*

Therefore, it is an illusion if we think that the relationship between manager and employee is power-free. As a continuation of this point, we can discuss how the ideal of a symmetrical relationship can be effectively followed. Why should managers have to exercise this style of leadership? In fact, why be a manager at all? Managers must attempt to create this symmetric relationship by making themselves into the ideal for their employees (Kirkeby, 2001), and therefore managers have to have practical strategies in order to accomplish their intentions. In the end it's about moving the employees in a particular direction (Lüscher & Staerk, 2008). In the above example, power still exists within the relationship, but it is an unspoken acknowledgement from both manager and employee. Power is still at work.

Another example of the indirect (modern) exercise of power is companies where work is organized into teamwork. In team-organization, coworkers put pressure on each other, instead of management having to directly put pressure on the employees. Other examples of the same form of hidden exercise of power are monitoring measures such as time registration, statistical inventory, and point systems. These are all technologies that many employees are familiar with in their everyday working life (Lüscher & Staerk, 2008).

Stelter (2002, p. 13) emphasizes indirect power in his understanding of coaching as a leadership tool: "Exploiting individual resources requires psychological support and time for learning, immersion, and development. It is here that coaching comes into the picture." Coaching is therefore a method of exploiting the individual resources, which is language that clearly emphasizes the strategic aspect of coaching as a leadership tool. When a manager coaches, it is in a way free of power dynamics.

We can argue that managers do not lose the traditional form of power if the ideals from the postmodern leadership paradigm are used in accordance with strategic causes. Power is simply expressed differently than it was under the modern leadership paradigm. Therefore, it could be said that managers continue to commit to modern leadership, just in a postmodern wrapping. The postmodern ideals are simply used to help the manager's ideas and directives "go down more easily" with the employees.

On the one hand, postmodern leadership can result in a manipulative practice, if managers hold on to their own truths and attempt to force those truths onto their employees. A manager who strategically uses modern power will appear untrustworthy and non-transparent. On the other hand, modern power is a way to ensure that employees use their shared influence in a collaborative decision, because ownership increases effective problem-solving. But is it even possible to attempt to eliminate the traditional form of power? Some leadership theorists have attempted to erase the power difference in their understanding of leadership, but they most often end up describing a manager who functions only as a consultant, and not as a manager who provides organizational direction.

If we maintain that leadership is about obtaining a shared goal, we must use both paradigms in order to understand the functions of a leader. In the traditional understanding, a leader should first and foremost protect the organization's interests, secure goals, provide frameworks and direction, and ensure that employees work with the correct tasks. The postmodern form of leadership is a constructive supplement to this understanding, where employees with ownership and commitment also have a natural desire to work for the best of the organization. The postmodern leadership style is brilliant at carrying the employee perspective and developing that perspective so that employees do the best for themselves, their development, career, and therefore also the organization, *if* a shared direction is set and held.

In practice, many managers know the feeling of not succeeding as a leader if they don't also practice strategic skills and take visible responsibility. An example of this can be seen in the following thoughts of a manager who worked with a self-managing team:

> Maybe I should talk to the employees in the production team individually if I want them to work better and more effectively together. But that will not result in more autonomy. Am I the one who should solve their collaboration difficulties, or should they? ... They should be responsible for solving their own conflicts. But will they do it? And what if they don't? I am still employed to be responsible for effectiveness. So I can't just let them figure it out on their own.
>
> Lüscher (2012, p. 175)

The postmodern leadership paradigm is so popular, and the emotional relationships in a company control so much, that we often experience managers who feel as if their most important task is to ensure that individual employees experience meaning and connection in their work. Those tasks that relate to the manager seeing what needs to happen in order for the organization to succeed can therefore be put on the back burner. What if you pushed your visions on someone, and they therefore lost their engagement and motivation? The reason for this problem is thinking in terms of "either-or": Either the manager controls the employees, and therefore the employees lose motivation, or the team is autonomous and therefore loses a shared feeling of direction.

The same example shows that the fact that the postmodern leadership paradigm can exist alongside the modern paradigm can impede a leader's understanding of his or her role. How can you be a leader in a context that demands that you both provide direction and delegate as well as that you lead and create self-management? This creates huge demands on the leader to create meaning from these contradictions.

On the bridge: leadership between paradigms

As a leadership consultant who works with developing, educating, and supporting managers, I see that the modern leadership paradigm is still dominant within today's organizations, at least in Scandinavian countries. I can also see that the appreciative approach from the postmodern paradigm has gained ground, and managers are expected to support and coach their employees. This is also reflected in educational programs and leadership courses, which primarily focus on training relationship and personal skills. Managers are trained how to use emotional, engaged methods in order to help their employees feel recognized, appreciated, and heard. However, as we have seen, organizational clarity and visibility can be created by combining the postmodern point of view with a modern leadership style. This will allow managers to keep focus on organizational and strategic skills, while still maintaining equality, relationship skills, and motivational skills. This combination can hopefully achieve the core task of leadership: creating shared direction and scope for employees. In other words, managers must embrace an understanding of the complexity, ambiguity, contradiction, and constant tension within their discipline.

If we are aware of the fact that managers must exist and act in a context of both modern and postmodern demands and ideals, it is possible to relate to this context and create balance between these contradictory paradigms. Postmodern leadership combined with modern demands creates a field of complexity, paradox, and ambivalence. This demands intense work with leadership positions in order to create framework, direction, and scope that gains and develops commitment from employees.

Managers who find themselves negotiating the tension between two concepts of leadership need a context where they can create meaning, direction, and connection in their leadership practice. The tensions between leadership concepts can include: the directive/authoritative versus the appreciative leadership form, the traditional visible power versus the invisible modern power, the visible leadership style versus the autonomous style, and the framework-providing style versus the coaching style.

We must understand leadership as a paradoxical task, where managers are stretched between demands (Table 2.2).

If we understand organizations as social contexts that are constantly changing in regard to challenges, transformations, tasks, and leadership needs, we must be more flexible and move across paradigms in order to find a leadership behavior that will be useful in relation to the organization's current status. Paradoxical leadership as a concept is related to a reflective relationship rather than an actual directive of good leadership. Paradoxical leadership, which we will explore in the second half of the book, means using both columns in Table 2.2. This requires a reflection about which position is best to use according to the organization's status and strategy as well as the internal leadership situation.

What should leadership use to navigate in practice? How do you connect the two paradigms? The initially seemingly incompatible approaches to leadership must be simultaneously at play, which means that managers must continually consider the following questions: Which situations are currently relevant in the organization/

TABLE 2.2 The modern versus the postmodern manager

Modern manager	*Postmodern manager*
"I must be visible"	"I must engage"
"I must make the decisions"	"I must motivate"
"I must go first and lead"	"I must stay behind and support"
"I must show the direction"	"I must reach out"
"I must take responsibility"	"I must give responsibility"
"I must know how to act"	"I must appreciate, ask, and listen"

department/team? In which direction do we want to move the company? Where is the organization/department/team in relation to these goals at the moment? And which leadership position would therefore be appropriate? Three different ways of relating to this paradox are presented in Chapters 10, 11, and 12. In these chapters I describe how you as a manager can integrate the two points of view and work using a leadership concept that builds a bridge between the paradigms.

Chapter summary

In this chapter I have indicated that there is a need to move away from the concept of "good leadership." Our understanding of good leadership comes from the fact that we commit ourselves to one paradigm and think about leadership from that perspective. I have critically examined the most popular leadership paradigm (the postmodern) and advocated that some of the modern leadership theories should once again be a part of our collective understanding of good leadership.

> **REFLECTIONS: WHICH PARADIGM DO YOU USE?**
>
> 1. Which paradigm does leadership lean toward most in your company?
> 2. What consequences does that have for your role as a manager?
> 3. What are the important leadership virtues to you?
> 4. Which assumptions do you have about what motivates your employees?
> 5. Which opportunities and limitations do you see in your way of understanding employee motivation?

In the rest of this book you will be introduced to a variety of relationship options that will make it possible for you to juggle tools and understandings from both paradigms, and thereby enrich your leadership practice.

3
THE LEGO PROJECT
An encounter with leadership's paradoxes

This chapter is structured as a narrative about an action research project that I completed several years ago. The narrative illustrates some of the organizational ambiguities, contradictory understandings, and double communications that are connected to organizational change. Paradoxes can clearly been seen within the organizational processes of change. As you read the chapter, you may find that some of the paradoxes can be a useful way of thinking in relation to your leadership tasks.

The narrative provides an idea about how paradoxes were created as a response to a group of people struggling with complexity in their organizations, ambiguous expectations, and ambivalence in regard to new ways of leading. As we will see, paradoxical thinking was created through dialog about the countless unsolvable situations that the managers experienced.

Narrative about an action research project

In 2002 I completed a three year research project that I had worked on in connection with the Business and Social Sciences program at Aarhus University and 45 managers from Lego's supply chain. The goal of the project was to investigate good leadership practice in connection with organizational change. At that time, Lego was involved in a significant process of change. In 1998, some months before my project began, growth had stagnated, the market was taken over by the competition, and Lego had hired a new CEO, Poul Plougmann. His task was to work with the owner, Kjeld Kirk Kristiansen, in order to create a strategy for how Lego could once again grow and distinguish itself in the market. As we look back on this goal, there can be many opinions about why Lego waited to implement these processes. However, regardless of when the changes happened, or who instigated them, the interesting aspect of the Lego project is that in the years between 1999 and 2003, the company went through fundamental organizational and commercial changes in order to create a platform for growth. These changes naturally led to the need for leadership changes.

When Poul Plougmann arrived in the company, he introduced a number of changes that were partially in conflict with the fundamental spirit of Lego. For the first time, Lego formed strategic alliances with Lucasfilm, McDonald's, and IBM, and other companies. This strategy had never before been a part of Lego. In addition, Lego's product line was transformed from the central Lego block to a fundamental element for constructing more technically complex toys. Lego became a new platform as a toy-giant, especially in the United States, where the concept of Mindstorms became a success.

This change required organizational changes in the supply chain. The number of employees and managers was reduced, and a change in leadership style was called for. The goal was high employee involvement, and this was to be accomplished through autonomous teams with high drive and responsibility for making decisions.

The Lego managers and I agreed that I would function as a consultant for them, and in return I would have free access to data for my research project. In practice, this meant that the managers used me as a sounding-board, coach, and process consultant, and that I used the data (obviously in an anonymous form) for my project.

This data was qualified by the fact that I had a focus group of eight managers who took part in regular meetings where we discussed some of the patterns and concepts that I developed along the way. In the focus group, we tested my assumptions, and together we investigated what was relevant to the manager role under such significant organizational change. I participated in rich conversations and meetings as well as process consultant work and observations of managers in practice. This allowed me to identify leadership challenges and potential methods of tackling these challenges.

As I have stated earlier, I wanted to get closer to the leadership challenges that were relevant in connection to the organizational changes. The entire Lego project has been published as a book titled *Working Through Paradox* (Lüscher, 2011). In this chapter, I will only use excerpts and the more practically applicable finds from my project, rather than the investigative methods and theoretical elements.

Long before I realized that my own thesis would be about paradoxes, and that the Lego managers were in danger of facing a number of leadership paradoxes related to organizational change, I noticed that almost all of the walls at Lego had a sign with a yin/yang symbol and text that described Lego's 11 leadership paradoxes. I discovered that the author of these paradoxes was the previous HR director, Per Sørensen, who had developed the 11 paradoxes together with senior management in 1985. These paradoxes were formulated as expectations for good leadership behavior for all levels of management. I asked Per Sørensen why these expectations were formulated as paradoxes and his answer was:

> You see, they came up because there was a lot of confusion among our top managers in regard to what we actually demanded, and what we should

demand of our managers further down in the organization. We wanted to do everything at the same time. It was an impossible task, but we agreed that they should be broadly oriented. They should have many competences, but they should also be able to differentiate between which competences should be used in which situation. I often use the plumber metaphor: He pipes hot and cold water into the house, but he never pipes lukewarm water. And we need managers who can make the water cool or warm depending on what is needed in the situation. I'm talking about a manager who is able to act in a way that is apparently contradictory, but is able to do it because it is necessary. A manager must know, cognitively, intuitively, and emotionally, when he should turn on which tap.

Personal interview, August 1999

The process which produced these paradoxical demands for the Lego managers is described in the book: *Lego: A Company and Its Soul* (*Lego-en virksomhed og dens sjael*) (Thygesen-Poulsen, 1993). The book describes, among other things, a senior management meeting that discussed how to create consistent demands of the managers in an organization:

There were simply no boundaries for what a manager should be able to do. Every action was included.
"He should be able to go in front," said one person.
"Yeah, and to stay in the background," added another.
Everyone laughed. Suddenly everyone was talking at the same time. The air was full of paradoxes.
"He should be dynamic!"
"Yeah, and thoughtful."
"Yeah, managers who have lofty ideals and who are well-functioning don't grow on trees!"
Small, fragrant smoke-rings rose from Kjeld Kirk Kristiansen's pipe. The process was really in motion now. HR director Per Sørensen went to the blackboard and began to organize the many opinions. The result was the 11 paradoxes that are now seen in every manager's office.

Thygesen-Poulsen (1993, p. 12)

Lego's 11 leadership paradoxes

As stated, the result of the meeting was 11 leadership paradoxes. They look like this:

The 11 paradoxes apply to all Lego managers, who must:

1) Establish close contact with their subordinates – and keep an appropriate distance,
2) Lead the way – and recede in the background,

3) Show confidence in their subordinates – and supervise,
4) Be open-minded – and normative,
5) Fight for their own unit – and submit to company objectives,
6) Plan their time – and be accessible,
7) Be direct in expressing their views – and be restrained,
8) Be visionary – and keep their feet on the ground,
9) Aim at consensus – and be able to cut through,
10) Be dynamic – and thoughtful and patient,
11) Be self-assured – and humble.

Per Sørensen, former personnel director at Lego

In 1987 these paradoxes were illustrated with a yin/yang symbol, which was meant to illustrate that it was expected that managers could balance apparently contradictory patterns of behavior in their leadership role. Leadership should be understood as a balancing of contradictory demands.

Although the 11 paradoxes were a formalized part of the organization, there were no actual initiatives taken to implement them in the organization. I noticed them in connection with my research project, due to the fact that they fit perfectly with the discoveries that I had made.

Managerial issues

In 1998, Lego announced a large organizational transformation process. The intention was that Lego should look at its organization and marketing situation in an entirely new way. In the supply chain this meant that managers would now be managing more employees (the manager staff was reduced from 72 to 45), which meant that they would be managing autonomous teams. The goal was to get employees involved, and create so much ownership, initiative, and involvement, that every single Lego employee would experience meaning and connection in their work, while simultaneously developing ambition.

When the project started in 1999, I interviewed all the managers and directors of the supply chain, as well as the employee representatives. These interviews contributed to the formation of a focus group that worked together in order to create an overview of what managers experienced as especially challenging during the initial stage of the process.

Some of the statements that were repeated or chosen by the focus group as particularly representative were:

- What is expected of me? I was chosen to be manager in the new organization based on my success in the old one. But now I need to succeed in something completely different…
- How do I set clear boundaries for the employees when they should also be autonomous? What do I make decisions about and what should I leave up to them?

- The danger is also that if we become more efficient at this level, is there then a need for me?
- I'm trying to change my manager role, but I don't know if it is in the right direction. How do you get support? I am also competing with the other managers right now.
- As a manager should you know everything yourself? I think that it is hard to involve people in decisions without appearing indecisive.
- It is a challenge to make our own management team function. We have been promoted due to our individual presentations. But now we are supposed to use our management team to share our insecurities.
- Many managers are ambivalent about the team-thinking approach. We do want to be in a community and do things together, but we also want to be independent and competent at the same time.

The managers struggled to improve and move toward presenting better results, and to manage considerably more employees. Furthermore, in times where things were changing rapidly and anxiety was high, it was difficult to experiment with new roles. The temptation to revert to well-known routines was intense. In an initial interview in August 1999, a production manager described his situation:

> It is difficult to make progress in this organization. Administration and technical problems take up all of our time. But that is not the only problem. When you are under pressure it is easier to do things that you know you are good at. And when it comes to this, most of us are, after all, technicians. Maybe we don't understand fully what it takes to be a manager in the new organization, and therefore we don't think so much about it. We just don't have the extra energy that it takes to think about it.
>
> Lüscher (2012)

The managers did not have any problems understanding the fundamental idea and strategy for these changes. However, creating meaning regarding the concrete issues they faced was something completely different. The managers knew where the organization should go, but they were unsure how that should be reflected in their leadership practice.

Many of the managers' questions and uncertainty were similar to the issues that I had experienced in other organizations where I had worked as a consultant. The managers had gained numerous leadership tools through seminars and courses, and they had the education and knowledge, but they still had an unspoken question: How could this knowledge and set of tools be translated into practice? The managers were very interested in this question. They experienced a paradoxical situation where the more turbulent, dynamic, and confusing the organization became, and the greater the need for oversight and meaning became, the less time they had to create the oversight and meaning that was demanded.

The shared goal of the Lego managers and my project was clear: we shared an interest in creating meaning in the complexity, ambiguity, and ambivalence that was found in an organization experiencing transformation, and we were together searching for ways to create more workable certainty and changed leadership behavior.

Brainstorming: conversation toward paradox

In order to help the managers, an implementation center was established, where managers could find a consulting partner and engage in productive conversations in order to develop their leadership practice. They could also find help in meetings with their colleagues and leadership team. The set-up for this implementation center is described in the book, *Working Through Paradox* (Lüscher, 2011).

In the following section, I will describe the brainstorming process further, show the model that we used in the brainstorming sessions, and provide an example of an interview with a manager. The conversation form that we used in this interview uses paradoxical thinking in order to form a pattern in which a chaotic task is transformed into an understanding of the complexities in the problem. The model also shows how we start with confusion, progress into the formulation of a dilemma, and end with finding a way to manage the paradox. The structure and work-methods of the model are perhaps most relevant for consultant colleagues, but as a manager I hope that you can see yourself reflected in the process.

The brainstorming sessions provided a framework for the meaning-creation processes, which in turn produced the option for managers to develop and transform their understandings of their leadership initiatives. According to Weick (1995), the "sensemaking-process" (the meaning-creation reflection process) is a process that attempts to transform small thoughts into large thoughts:

> Words induce stable connections, establish stable entities to which people can orient…Agreement on a label that sticks is as constant a connection as is likely to be found in organizations.
>
> *Weick (1995, p.128)*

The brainstorming sessions attempted to facilitate the meaning-creation process through emphasizing subtle details in the managers' narrative, working with them, providing them with new perspectives, and helping them see themselves in a new light. This allowed the manager to find new ways to act. It is the consultant's job to attempt to create an appropriate disruption in the manager's perspectives. This allows the consultant and manager to work together in order to investigate how they can change their understandings of the issues.

Weick (1995) claims that questioning our own assumptions and frames of reference is a discipline that places large demands on the individual. However, he also states that, most of the time, we think about issues in the same way we usually do. Our system has a tendency to recognize patterns and problems, which results in

32 Paradoxical leadership as a way of thinking

habitual action. This saves energy, since we don't spend energy on unfamiliar situations. The problem for Lego was that they were facing such huge changes that their habitual way of thinking about management needed to be replaced with something new. Therefore, there was a need to create a reflective space, and this was done through brainstorming sessions.

The model below shows how the process operated by creating more clarity from the contradictory demands on managers. The process starts with a problem, a question, a confusion, or sometimes an attitude that the manager brings with them. A colleague has also called this a "movement wish," and in the model it is called "the mess." In the following section, I will use an example to describe how Lego managers worked toward a paradoxical understanding of their own problems. I will use the managers' feelings of chaos and ignorance as a starting point for my explanation. The model for our consulting conversations is illustrated in Figure 3.1.

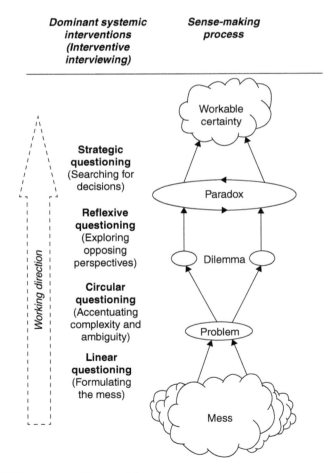

FIGURE 3.1 The sense-making model

The brainstorming sessions at Lego most often started with a manager presenting a theme or area of concern, or where there was something that he or she found difficult regarding leadership. We subsequently called this "something" "mess," since "mess" was characteristic of many different thoughts and issues. We could recognize a theme on the overall level, but couldn't find a concrete issue. Through questions, we then began to formulate a problem together. This could also be viewed as the introductory contract for the conversation, where the manager and consultant agree on what the manager wants to work with, ensure that they both have understood the problem, and agree on how to proceed as well as what is the expected outcome of the conversation. Linear questions are used in order to investigate what is happening in the manager's practice and to clarify the manager's understanding of the potential connections and stumbling-blocks within the problem.

The next phase of the model questions the manager's understandings, delves into more detail, and unpacks the problem. The leader often formulates the dilemmas of the problem with the help of coaching. When the manager is able to see the contradictory demands that challenge his or her solution, he or she is then able to formulate a dilemma. We found that when the conversation moved between general demands and single aspects of the issue, or when we tried potential scenarios for solving both sides of the dilemma, we were "cast" back to the opposite issue, and therefore discovered that the issue was not so mutually exclusive after all. We weren't talking about a difficult choice, as the dilemma stipulated, but rather about a paradox, which required that both opposing understandings and demands were simultaneously present. The next section will look closer at the movement that produced the paradox.

The mess

A postmodern viewpoint of how we convincingly describe reality is defined by the way we relate to reality. For example, if you are going to a party and focus on meeting the guests you have a good relationship with, you will look forward to the party. As a result, you will come into the party in a festive and positive mood, which you know you and your friends will appreciate. On the other hand, if you look at the guest list and see that there are a lot of people coming who you don't know, and that on top of that you have to sit at Aunt Olga's table and will therefore be expected to "get the party going," you will relate to the event in a different way. You might anticipate that you won't have so much fun at your table, and therefore arrange for a taxi to pick you up early ("just in case it gets boring"), but still wonder if it might be fun after all, and end up debating whether you should stay later, etc. You can choose to pay attention to a wide variety of factors for any given event. The way you regard a situation will determine which solutions and plans of action you will have available. Each situation has various elements that will contribute to how you process the situation.

There are many ways in which managers can formulate "the mess" found in leadership tasks. Ackhoff (1985), who works with creating reflections with managers, has called this first part of reflective leadership "formulating the mess." This is the first step in helping managers discuss and form reflections about their managerial tasks. "Formulating the mess" means emphasizing one thing over others, as well as clarifying and limiting which part of the complex problem you intend to work with.

This process of constructing a clear relation to the issue creates a continuous limitation, which provides clarity. As Weick states,

> People seem to need the idea that there is a world with Peruvian features of ready-made information, because to give up this idea of the world as a fixed and stable reference point is to fall into idealism, nihilism, or subjectivism, all of which is unseemly.
>
> Weick (1995, p. 37)

In other words, ascribing order to the world doesn't simply mean interpreting the world, but instead becoming the author of the world. "Sense-making" (creating meaning in the world) is about re-writing just as much as interpreting. It's about creating as well as uncovering. Therefore, through "formulating the mess," the manager creates a foundation from which we can explore complexity, ambiguity, and ambivalence. The Lego managers often waited for senior management to formulate "the mess," since this was often perceived as being connected to the change within the organization. The managers wanted senior management to be clearer in regard to goals, visions, strategies, economic frameworks, etc. However, they still found senior management to be ambiguous, which led to a high level of frustration.

Due to this shared feeling of frustration with the system, the managers began to use brainstorming sessions in order to discuss and attempt to solve their own experiences of complex, ambiguous, and impossible situations. The conversations were used to create a sense of meaningful order and structure, and allowed the managers to accept the social reality that the organization consisted of a mess of complex relationships between fragmented information, experience, etc. The process of creating meaning was aided by the addition of an initial (although oversimplified) order to the mess.

For example, a conversation could start with a "fluffy" and open question such as "How do we start to work as a team?" or "What are the expectations from senior management regarding…?" This type of question reflects the managers' desire for a simple answer to a complicated question. The open question was the first step toward formulating the mess. The managers were already starting the process of explaining the theme to themselves and the consultant.

The idea of the brainstorming sessions can be seen as a way to work toward bringing the manager out of the mess by figuratively providing order and a way to structure the mess. Bateson (in Ølgaard, 2004) has used the word "punctuation" to describe the way in which we choose parts of the information stream and then formulate that information using language that allows us to discuss and form reflections about the information. The purpose of this first phase of the conversation is to explore which parts of the mess/information stream the manager wants to focus on, and therefore begin to form a shared idea about which theme the manager and consultant should work on within the conversation. Benedicte Madsen has written an article, "Mess and Cleanup in Organizations" ("Rod og oprydning i organisationen") (1998), where she states that the role of the consultant is to contribute to mental clean-up as well as to create an overview of the organization as a complex system. She also states that the idea behind this is that it is better for the employees to have an overview of the mess involved in the organization than it is for them to lack an overview and remain ignorant as to the state of the mess.

The formulation of the mess pulls the manager out of the mess. However, the formulation of the mess does not yet define the problem. Therefore, the next step is to explore the theme which has been formulated in order to linguistically "frame it" and give it a workable name.

It can be useful for managers to use this method of thinking about conversations, both informally with colleagues as well as in leadership team meetings. Being available and asking interested questions allows managers to help each other create clarity and the drive to act. In the following section, I provide an example of the formulation of a problem. I was the one asking the questions, but it would have been just as effective if the conversation had taken place between two colleagues.

The problem

A problem can be defined as the relationship between the individual who "has the problem," and the preferences of the individual. A problem is characterized by the fact that there is disharmony between reality and one's own preferences. The problem is not a physical entity, but a mental construction, and therefore the conversation must treat the problem as a mental construct. In other words, there is something rather arbitrary about formulating something as a problem: You formulate it in a certain way, and when you make a situation problematic, you set your agenda for future attention and problem-solving.

In the Lego project, I used questions that were about limiting and understanding the problem in order to help the manager to simplify, limit, and formulate the theme as a question or problem. Here is an example:

A manager formulated the following question: "I have a very prestigious product-development project in my department. I picked out a manager to be responsible for it, but how can I be sure that he chooses the right team of employees to work with him?"

This introductory question was very broad, and the context of the question was still very unclear. I used the following question to explore why this was problematic for him:

LL: Why is this important to you?
MANAGER: Because I am responsible, and I have all the experience. I know people better than he does.

LL: What is your explanation for choosing him as project leader, rather than choosing yourself?
MANAGER: Because he has a better sense of this type of project than I do.
LL: Ah, so you know who can do the job best, but he knows what should be done for the project? Is that the case?
MANAGER: Yeah, but I let him choose the team, because I want to make him more responsible. But I'm not sure that the person he chose to be his right-hand man for the project was a good choice.
LL: Why not?
MANAGER: I've had some experience with him. He can't solve things, he's not so reliable.
LL: Why don't you say that to him?
MANAGER: I have, but he said that he thought that the guy would be better this time because it's a different type of project.
LL: And as I understand it, you have a problem with …

The conversation continued until the following section:

LL: If you were to formulate the problem a bit more simply, maybe as a question, how would you formulate it?
MANAGER: That I want to work with how I can feel comfortable with my project leader choosing the right people for this project.

When he heard himself formulate the problem, it became clearer which part of the complex theme we should work with.

The dilemma

When the manager has formulated his or her theme as a problem (an oversimplified version of how he or she sees the theme), we then investigate how he or she understands the problem. In this phase of the conversation we collaborate in order to discover various aspects of the problem, investigate how these aspects interact, and discover which factors might be relevant to solving the problem. In this phase, we use questions in order to uncover new perspectives and points of view that the manager hasn't considered before. This can be seen in the example below:

LL: What effect does it have on the project leaders below you when you make decisions about themes such as this?
MANAGER: Normally they just follow my decision. I think that I make the correct decisions, hahaha, so why shouldn't they follow them?
LL: And your manager, what does he think about the fact that it is you who makes these decisions?
MANAGER: Nothing, it's what I've always done. But he also expects that I delegate those types of decisions. Which means that I have to do it more and more.

LL: What about your colleagues, do they expect that you let them make decisions like these?
MANAGER: Yeah, that is also why I am hesitant. I have told them that I will delegate more decisions to them. But in this case, that is a problem – when I am ultimately responsible for the outcome on behalf of the department…
LL: Okay. If I understand this correctly, you get less out of your project-manager when it is you who makes the decisions, because he feels undervalued. Have I understood that correctly?
MANAGER: Yeah, I told him that he was responsible, but…
LL: But if you let him run the project and make decisions, would it get out of control and the project-manager would make the wrong decision, which would have consequences for the project?
MANAGER: Yes, exactly. So what can I do? I feel that the project will suffer if I relinquish control, and if I take control, the project will also suffer, but due to other reasons.

When we discussed the problem in depth, and considered it from additional angles, it led to a dilemma. The feeling of being in a dilemma creates a feeling of stagnancy, because the dilemma demands a choice with significant consequences, regardless of which choice is made. At this point in the conversation, I asked questions that were designed to place greater attention on the polarities and tensions that are connected with the problem, as well as to help the manager to take various alternatives into account.

The next section of the conversation focuses on filling out the narrative and bringing additional aspects to light. We investigated the problem as well as possible meanings and opinions before we moved on.

LL: What has been the project-manager's reason for choosing this other person as his right-hand man?
MANAGER: He believes that this person has many original ideas and is very intelligent.
LL: What do you think about his explanations? Do they make sense to you?
MANAGER: Not at all. I mean, yes, I usually see it like that as well, but I am doubtful because of the experiences I have had with him.
LL: Do you think that he could handle it if he got another chance?
MANAGER: He has already had a lot of chances…or no, I mean, I think that I don't really know. But I don't really want to take the risk.

This example shows how we can investigate the complexity of a situation by examining different perspectives (the manager's, the employee's, the organization's, etc.). We can already begin to construct the paradox through a close investigation of the dilemma. Continuing to work with the dilemma results in the manager's realization that the problem can be understood as an "either-or" problem, but that making a decision will not remove the problem or ease the tension (Bartunek, 1988; Lewis, 1999; Westenholz, 1999).

Many experiments and studies have shown that when managers formulate their problem as a dilemma, they use language in order to avoid controlling the contradictory aspects of the solution, and that they avoid the more emotional problems. This was also the case in my study. All of the different types of responses I received regarded something other than relating to complexity, ambiguity, and ambivalence. This, as in so many other broad processes regarding change, resulted in the creation of counter-reactions in the places where meaning wasn't found.

In the Lego project, we noticed three forms of defensive responses to being in an extremely complex situation. The first was an oversimplification along the lines of: "What is the problem? You could just do this and this." This type of response has to do with negotiation. Managers who reacted in this way wanted to shut down the complexity and ambiguity by resorting to quick solutions.

The second type of response that we met was denial. These managers typically said something along the lines of: "I usually do this, and it has brought me to where I am today, it has always worked, so therefore I will continue doing it. That's the way I am!" This response is also a way of reacting to and avoiding complexity.

The third type of response was to hold the problem at arm's length in order to completely distance oneself from the challenges of the problem. An example could be: "Senior management has to realize that we can't implement the team-thinking approach when we also have to produce certain results. They have to decide what they want, and there isn't much we can do before they do that."

All three types of response typically arose at the point where the manager "met" complexity and realized that the solution wasn't immediately apparent. It was here where we continued to investigate various complex aspects of the issue, regardless of our frustration.

The paradox: realizing connections

In my conversation with the Lego managers, the dilemma did not lend itself to any simple solutions. In our conversations we began to investigate the possible consequences of a decision, and this made the contradictions even more apparent. To use Argyris's concept of "double loop-learning" (1995), managers began to question their own approach and previous understanding of the problem. The double loop concept refers to the process by which a manager progresses to a higher level of investigation, in that he or she begins to juggle additional ways of understanding the problem. Let us return to the case of the manager who had difficulty giving control to his project-manager:

MANAGER: I'm stuck, because I am responsible for this decision. And it isn't possible. He knows that I have to let him be responsible for his own presentations, just like everyone else. But how can I vouch for and be responsible for the consequences?

LL: Let's return to something you said earlier about being responsible for the project-manager's decision. Is it always like that, or just in relation to this guy that it is a problem?

MANAGER: Yeah, it's actually always like that, we have to delegate more than we are used to, but we still have the overall responsibility...

LL: So can you explain how it all fits together? What does responsibility mean? Is it something that doesn't fit in your role, or does it make sense when seen in the larger picture?

MANAGER: I mean, I can see that people perform better if they make the decisions themselves. I am the same way. The more you say to me about what I should do, the less I care.

LL: It sounds like you want to let the project-manager make the decision. But are you worried about the consequences if you do that?

MANAGER: Yeah, it is important for me to show my project-manager that I trust him, but I just don't agree with his decision. It's probably something to do with the fact that I have to let go and yet still have control at the same time...

LL: Yeah, it sounds that way to me too...

Later in the Lego project, we realized that the paradoxical way of thinking was helpful in itself. The contradictions and dilemma were given new meaning, and after a while, the manager began to incorporate the polarities into the dilemma. We realized that a new form of logic was beginning to materialize for the manager. These new connections were sometimes very apparent to me as a brainstorming partner. As a result, I could be surprised when the manager suddenly saw the connection as something special. However, there were other moments where the connection that was made in the conversation was so new to me that my way of thinking was also challenged.

When solutions in the form of a choice between contradictory solutions or options began to show themselves to be absurd, we realized that both solutions needed to be a part of the managerial decision. We often found that we needed to work with understanding or reformulating the problem in order to make sure it included the apparently contradictory options. As a result, the focus group began to question the "either-or" thinking that the managers often had when they first approached us with the intention of brainstorming. Together, we began to develop the idea that the apparently mutually exclusive "either-or" solutions could often develop into "both-and" solutions. Both polarities needed to be included in the leadership role, and the art was to do both simultaneously.

In other words, the conversations showed that the paradox first appears as a feeling of absurdity and/or paralysis. This is caused by the realization that while elements of our thoughts, actions, and emotions appear logical when considered independently, they appear absurd when considered together.

In the example above, we discussed the paradox that we later called the control-and-trust paradox. The manager now seemed to be positive and ready to concentrate. He began to juggle alternative ways to act in regard to his problem.

LL: If you were to describe this project for me, as it would be in five months, when everything has been solved, what would you say?

MANAGER: I would say that I was glad that I had listened to the project-manager, because the other guy has surprised me and thrown some brilliant ideas into the project, haha!
LL: And what would you say made that possible?
MANAGER: That I took the chance and trusted him.
LL: Which means that you showed trust. But how did you keep control so that you could ultimately be responsible for the result?
MANAGER: [long pause] I think, I asked him to keep me oriented about how the guy was doing. And then to be willing to act quickly if it wasn't working. Listen, I totally agree that I have to let go of control, but at the same time I need to find ways to keep control.

Workable certainty

In the Lego project, the managers wanted to find ways to create meaning and action in a complex process of organizational changes. They attempted to do this through escaping the paralysis of paradox. The conversations we had were an attempt to reduce complexity, minimize ambiguity, and understand the demands and expectations of senior management more clearly.

The managers' desire for clarity and order temporarily resulted in a paradoxical effect on our brainstorming sessions. As a result of our conversations, their problems were experienced as more complex, rather than simple and without ambiguity.

According to Weick,

> the manager makes sense of information and actions in order to **create a workable certainty** for organizational members. Thus, these authors all emphasize organizational communication and negotiation toward a shared reality as fundamental to workable certainty. Rather than precise judgement of external or objective facts, organizational actors socially construct the shared organizational reality to form a basis for action.
>
> *Weick (1969, pp. 41–42)*

In the Lego project, we could also see how the manager began to create a "landing" for his problem in the moment that he had identified the ambiguous and paradoxical elements of the situation. The solution contained the paradox and provided the opportunity for new questions to be asked and answered in relation to both polarities of "the dilemma."

Weick calls this a movement toward "workable certainty." The concept refers to the fact that we can never have full control and unambiguous understanding of the information and demands that we meet. The sense-making process (the process by which we attribute meaning to our actions and the information available) is an ongoing process. Therefore, it must not be mistaken for a process where we have full knowledge and control over what will happen and how it happens, but instead as a process which reduces complexity and ambiguity just enough so that we can find our way to understanding and potential action.

In the Lego project, the movement toward workable certainty was reflected by the fact that the manager had new energy and optimism, and began to see options and formulate new questions/tasks for himself. Afterwards, we realized that the paradox was often contained in the new questions/new perspective regarding the problem. As shown below, we did not find simple solutions, but instead gained enough oversight to make action possible.

LL: Okay, let's look at what we can do right now. What you're saying points toward the future, but is it also realistic to implement? I think that you want to give him control, but you also know that you don't want to let go of your control. How does that make sense?

MANAGER: It makes sense. I have to do both. But if I want to give him more control and still maintain control, he needs to share information with me. I will need to know that it's going like it should.

LL: What does that mean for you now?

MANAGER: I think that I need to discuss this more with my project-manager. Maybe I should let him make the decision, and then make sure that there are regular meetings where he reports to me about how the project is going. And then, if it doesn't go well, we can change the decision.

LL: What effect will that have on the project-manager?

MANAGER: I don't know…I hope that he won't feel too controlled by me…

LL: I think so too. If you watch all of the steps he takes, you risk being just as controlling anyway. How would he react if you share some of these thoughts with him? If you say that you really want to show him trust, but are unsure about what will happen in the project? If you tell him that you want to show him trust and still maintain control?

MANAGER: I think he would understand that. Maybe, if he really understands, I could even ask him what we would suggest we do in order for me to show trust but still feel like I am in control.

The brainstorming session ended here. I have used it here to show several things. First, the case shows how we worked with brainstorming as a part of meaning-creation with the managers. This part is not so relevant in the context of this book, but the other aspects are important. Second, it shows how a leadership problem can move from an "either-or" problem to a "both-and" problem throughout the course of a brainstorming session. Third, it provides an example of how managers begin to formulate their leadership challenges in paradoxical terms. This provided them with the opportunity to avoid solving the problem in a problem→solution context, but instead choose to incorporate complexity and create workable certainty for a problem that was just as complex, but more concrete.

The brainstorming sessions led to the managers' realization that thinking in terms of one-dimensional solutions was no longer an option. We felt obliged to find complex solutions to complex problems. We found that an ending in the form of a "result" was not seen as an option. We preferred something that was more of a "manageable mess" instead.

Naturally, it is difficult to recognize the paradox in a problem and take it seriously. When paradoxes are seen as paralytic, it is difficult to know how a manager can manage them. The conversation process that is illustrated in this chapter shows what often happens in the process of recognition: our brains automatically reject dilemmas. Think of all the times you have been stuck in a dilemma and couldn't act, because any action would cost too much either way. Dilemmas are difficult situations, where you experience an "either-or" choice with significant consequences either way. How often have you stood in the shower, gone jogging, or are in the middle of a meeting and suddenly think of a solution which actually incorporates both sides of the dilemma? It is here that you meet the paradox. You find a solution that incorporates both polarities, often in the form of a creative solution, and you suddenly see the problem completely differently. Brainstorming and conversations with colleagues can also do this, if you look for ways to handle the paradox.

The Lego example has two important points:

- Managerial reflection, preferably with colleagues or a coach, is a useful way to create a little more oversight and certainty in complex and contradictory situations. This can lead to the ability to find "both-and" solutions that match the complexity of the problem, without reducing complexity or the paradox.
- The Lego project is an example of a leadership paradox that illustrates how paradox is a way of thinking. This way of thinking often occurs when you are in the process of reflecting about how you should lead.

With these movements toward paradox in mind, we will now examine three types of paradoxes that I found after countless conversations, meetings, focus group meetings, and interviews with the Lego managers. The three types of paradoxes that the Lego managers and I identified are:

1. The organizational paradox. This type of paradox could also be called the change paradox. It is about the problems that are an inherent part of an organization, especially during a process of transformation. For example: the paradoxes between centralizing and decentralizing, autonomy and documentation, renewal and stability, focus on people and focus on results. The organizational paradox is a part of organizational life, but it is especially apparent when the organization is undergoing change, as there is an immediate need for stability *and* for change.
2. The role paradox. The role paradox deals with the leadership behavior that the Lego managers needed to show in order for a strategy to succeed. Should you take the lead or stay behind? Should you involve people in the process in order to increase efficiency, or should you just inform and set demands? The role paradox is mainly about which demands are made on the manager's leadership behavior.

3. The paradox of belonging. The paradox of belonging was the first to appear in the Lego project. It is about the interpersonal processes within the organization. And also much about mixed emotions. For example: the paradox between being individualistic and being a team player, the paradox between being loyal to management's decisions and feeling connected to employees, or the paradox between taking independent steps because autonomy is praised and simultaneously risking that those steps will be punished. The paradox of belonging is about operating within your emotional ambivalence, as well as recognizing the emotional ambivalence within yourself and your leadership team.

Summary

In the Lego project, the managers worked to create workable certainty when a problem was experienced as being fixed and difficult to solve. How should you act and how should you understand a problem with all of its complexity? The paradox perspective helped the managers to incorporate the "both-and" solutions of paradox, and to find solutions that only reduced complexity to the degree at which it was possible to find workable certainty.

REFLECTIONS: PARADOXES IN YOUR LEADERSHIP

1. Which contradictory demands are presented to you as a manager?
2. How often do you talk about the complexity and difficulties of solving strategic problems that you meet in the management team?
3. How often do you share that complexity with your colleagues?
4. Which of Lego's 11 paradoxes can you recognize in your daily work?
5. How do you work with these paradoxes?

The first section of the book has now introduced you to the need for applying paradox as a lens for leadership, options, and limitations. We have seen that this can be accomplished through thinking across leadership paradigms. You were also given an example of how paradoxes became relevant to my work with the Lego project.

In the second section of the book, we will attempt to understand the three types of paradoxes in greater depth. I will start by providing you with examples from Lego, and then give some concrete examples of how you can practically work with making sense of these paradoxes.

PART II
Paradoxical leadership development

4

THE ORGANIZATIONAL PARADOX

The paradox inherent in organizational life

All companies have fundamental "either-or" questions that, upon closer inspection, appear to be closely connected. Should we enter the new market now, or wait and see if the market is ready? Should we develop something new or rely on what we know? Should we change or stabilize ourselves? The answer is: yes! Organizations must manage both types of challenges simultaneously. For example, I have often worked in the creative sector, where innovation and "newness" are essential in order to become recognized, but at the same time, things can't be *so* different that they won't sell. We usually say that companies in the creative sector need to think outside the box, but within the framework. In order to create change, it is necessary to maintain a stable work environment within the company.

In order to accommodate the new, it is also necessary to have structure and habits that can manage what already exists. For example, when new managers are hired in a management team, they need to be in agreement with the spirit of the organization, but they must also complement the existing team members. Both uniformity and diversity are relevant. These many paradoxical demands on companies can be called organizational paradoxes, because they are conditions that are found in all organizations.

I will begin this chapter by using an example from Lego in order to introduce an understanding of organizational paradoxes. I will then introduce a tool, the Competing Values Framework, as a way of working strategically with organizational paradoxes during organizational change in order to create workable certainty.

Organizational paradoxes at Lego

Toward the end of the management development project at Lego, the focus group discussed a number of themes related to finding oneself in an organization in the midst of change. They had been in the process of change for a long time (three years), and the following questions had arisen from the start of the project: How do we create meaning in our own roles in the midst of all of these projects that had been developed in order to create change? How do we translate all of the contradictory demands into action? How can we understand complex and vague messages when senior management doesn't even know what they mean, but just continue to be vague and ambiguous? It turned out that organizational paradoxes were especially connected to the process of change, and that this type of paradox created an organizational "waiting-room atmosphere" because the direction of the organization was unclear. This is how it looked in the Lego project:

> One of the managers stated: "It is interesting that this is happening in the organization right now. I think that the managers are having a hard time creating meaning from it all. Nobody can work effectively when there is so much turbulence in the organization. It's as if we are just waiting for the changes to be over so that we can start to work…but yeah, I know that we are also a part of the change. But do we have to keep changing all the time – is that how it has to be, or should we create something more stable?
>
> In other words, the managers tried to understand the organization they were a part of, as well as the intentions behind the new complex processes of change. There was special focus on senior management and the vague communication that was coming from the top. The fact that the managers experienced contradictory demands from senior management created frustration, and senior management became the focus for the managers' experience of ambiguity and overall lack of oversight. The managers felt that senior management should explain the overall understandings, priorities, demands for presentation, and intentions behind the assignments they were given.
>
> I had a lively discussion with the managers about this topic. I reminded them of the large number of informational meetings and the total amount of information that had been shared during the time we had worked together. However, this information just increased their feelings of confusion, complexity and uncertainty. My impression was that the managers didn't know how they should interpret and translate the messages that were coming from senior management. The managers agreed with this, but attributed it to the lack of clarity from senior management. We continued to discuss whether ambiguity and frustration could be attributed to vague communication, or (as I argued) if ambiguity was a part of the process.
>
> Even though we did not manage to reach agreement on this topic, the energy from our discussions allowed me to begin to be able to distinguish between paradoxes that arise due to vague communication, and paradoxes that could perhaps be a part of the system and the process of change."

Several studies have shown that organizational changes create tension and contradictions (see Argyris, 1995; Poole & Van de Ven, 1989; Miller, 1983; Smith & Berg, 1987; Weick & Westley, 1999). For example, Putnam (1986) describes the built-in contradictions that arise between what exists and what the organization is moving towards. The organization creates frameworks for what is correct and what is incorrect in regard to achieving its goals. When you want to create organizational change, the new and the old will clash as you try to understand and evaluate the new approach using the frameworks of the existing approach. This results in the reproduction of the existing approach. Weick & Westley (1999) state that to learn is to disorganize and increase variation. Therefore, to organize is to reduce variation. In an attempt to focus on learning, theorists often overlook this tension between the new and the old. The forces between a stable organization and new ideas (which is a type of disorganization) need to be seen as opposites in order to understand the tension between them. Learning usually happens when new situations are investigated and new ways of organizing are explored. People are innovative, but at the same time we are able to understand that we must create and maintain identity while creating new frameworks. It is only when we juxtapose order and chaos, challenge and the use of what already exists, the old and the new, and only when we see the old and the new together, that we can create genuine change. In other words, something must be familiar and stable before we can step forward into something new.

The contradictions between the existing and the new were quite apparent at Lego. The managers began to investigate these tensions and therefore were able to begin to create meaning in the unavoidably contradictory messages that were a part of the process of change. For example, one of the managers attempted to create meaning from the fact that large organizational changes were needed in order to create a team structure and implement the education that employees would need to achieve this change. He experienced a paradox in that he needed to teach his employees to fit into a structure, even though this structure was undergoing constant change. His problem was that the large amount of changes resulted in the fact that he couldn't work with giving the employees a new "mindset," teach them to act differently, and teach them to understand what it meant to be an autonomous team all at the same time. Something had to wait. However, he also realized that the organization would only be changed once the employees acted differently, which could only happen as the result of a changed mindset. He called this paradox "the chicken or the egg." What came first, the organization's structure or the employees' education? Both parts were dependent on each other. We later referred to this as the stability-change paradox. Stability and change can be contradictory parts of an understanding of learning, but it is necessary that they are both in focus simultaneously, since each is a prerequisite for the other.

The stability-change paradox is not new. Democritus and Heraclitus vigorously debated whether the world should be understood according to structure (Democritus) or process (Heraclitus). The Lego managers were engaged in a lively discussion about whether they should maintain what already existed (existing policies, goals, and structures) or focus on involving human relations and social processes and challenging their employees. Action demanded a structure (with which to understand and create meaning) and structure could only be created through action.

Questions such as "Where are we going?" What do we want?" And "What is the goal/purpose?" can be asked, but not clearly, and not without contradictions. As a rule, you cannot say where an organization is going until it gets there. Therefore, we must act within the framework of the organization in order to create organizational change.

Communication: the system's contradictions

Organizational paradoxes are most often seen through poor communication, which can confuse managers and others in the organization. The paradoxes can be seen in the contradictions and messages that point in opposite directions. As soon as senior management introduces a change, employees and managers will find themselves under pressure to both maintain what already exists and to create something new. This can appear as though management is communicating ambiguously, and that is true. Each process of change must create meaning between the tensions of what exists and what is new, between old and new roles, and between the focus you have had to succeed and the focus you will need to establish.

An example of this could be the way Danish schools have recently worked with the concept of inclusion. Instead of removing children with learning or social difficulties from the classroom, the intention is to try to solve these problems within the classroom. This solution requires that teachers make an effort to intervene as soon as they realize that a child has special needs. However, at the same time, teachers have been informed that the learning level of their class needs to be improved, and that children need to learn more. Inclusion means that teachers have to spend more time with the children that need more time, and increased demand on performance means that teachers have to spend more time improving their students' performance and focusing on helping all of the students become better. There is a paradox in this situation: focus on the students that have the potential to improve *and* focus on the students who are not doing so well. It is therefore understandable that teachers and schools have to create meaning from these apparent contradictions before they can create a sensible plan for inclusion *and* academic performance.

This is but one example of the contradictions that can be found in systems, and the larger and more complex the system becomes, the more paradoxes will be found through communication.

During the Lego project, I interviewed Kjeld Kirk Kristiansen and Poul Plougmann regarding how they viewed the contradictory messages that had resulted in the organization's employees feeling paralyzed.

I found that Kjeld Kirk Kristiansen and Poul Plougmann themselves represented a paradox. Kjeld Kirk Kristiansen often talked about the importance of preserving the characteristics of the Lego-spirit. By this he meant that Lego was world-renowned for its blocks, and the values, simplicity, and creativity associated with the product, as well as the fact that Lego could set itself apart from most of the other toy companies because it stood alone, did not have alliances, and had always sold easily recognizable products. He thought that this should also be reflected internally, through the satisfaction, pride, and product-knowledge of employees, as well as a good team, which built on the fundamental values of previous years.

Poul Plougmann's interview represented a sharp contrast to this way of thinking. He talked about innovation regarding products, strategic alliances with other branches (film, fast food, IT, etc.), new and more effective forms of organization, trimming the organization, ways management could challenge employees, and incorporating modern technology, among other things.

As if it wasn't enough that managers and employees needed to keep quiet in order to find out what they should listen to, one director emphasized stability, and the other change. When the directors were asked about their apparently contradictory points of view, they answered that it was essential that both voices were heard in the organization. Kjeld Kirk Kristiansen and Poul Plougmann were both aware that the company would not survive in an "either-or," director-determined environment. Therefore, they felt that they needed to represent a balanced effort between change and stability. If everything was reconstructed, the company's history, strong brand, and customer recognition would disappear, but if they kept doing what they had been doing, the toy brand would slowly fall behind in relation to new markets, new forums, and new products.

Therefore, it is not so unusual that the managers experienced ambiguity from the communication from senior management. Table 4.1 shows the organizational paradoxes that the Lego managers experienced as contradictory.

If the managers sat around and waited for senior management to find out where they were going, the organization would fail, and the managers would then be justified in claiming that the new direction of the organization wasn't working. When the managers did not act in accordance with creating meaning and flow in their experiences of contradictions and paradox, senior management was forced to further develop their visions, goals, and strategies. Just like the managers of single departments waited for clarity from their immediate bosses, the bosses waited for clarity from senior management. Senior management was therefore again forced to communicate even more clearly and focus on only one dimension. Communication will end up in a self-strengthening pattern because the managers will once again experience that the "one-dimensional" and "clear" messages from senior management contain a long list of contradictions and lack of relevance.

When managers try to create stability, clarity, change, innovation, etc. all at the same, they will instead create a number of ambiguities which will be seen through managers feeling insecure and lacking a sense of direction. This insecurity must be addressed, and accepted, as a starting point for being able to act in the midst of ambiguity.

According to more philosophical paradox theories (e.g. Luhmann, Heraclitus, Dewey), it is not considered worthwhile to avoid paradoxes. Quite the opposite. In order for an organization's employees to maintain their skills throughout a process of change, paradoxes must be taken in their stride and accepted. This means that

TABLE 4.1 Organizational paradoxes

The problem →	The dilemma →	The paradox →	→ Toward workable certainty
How can I implement a team organization when my team is always changing?	Should I implement a new team now **or** wait until things calm down?	Change **and** stability	How can I implement a team that can be changed as needed?
How do we obtain more information from senior management?	Should I know what is going on around me **or** should I just know what concerns my department?	Fight for your own department **and** constantly think about the organization as a whole	I should ask for the information I need in order to make appropriate decisions regarding my own department.
Which themes are relevant to our work in leadership meetings?	Is our internal cooperation important **or** should we meet regarding the shared strategy?	Goal **and** process	How can we place our cooperation on the agenda in order to work together and reach our goals?
How can I work in accordance with the new organization when my employees aren't motivated? They think that it will just change again soon.	Should I introduce a new team organization **or** should I respect my employees' wishes?	People act according to what is meaningful **and** meaning is created through action	How can I work with motivation during this team organization process?
I need to organize a unit of 12 people, but there are 17 of us.	Should I follow "the rules" **or** should I decide based on what makes the most sense for my department?	Senior management: Don't do what we say!	I will do what is meaningful and then inform them that I have done something other than what they said.

acceptance must be a part of the process of change. This does not mean acceptance in its passive form, where we just wait around if nobody knows where we are going. Instead it means acceptance in the form of understanding that the organization's paradoxes are something which employees must relate to, especially during a process of change. Later we will discuss how you can work with organizational paradoxes and accept them as part of the strategic work of your organization.

A tool for strategic-change projects: Competing Values Framework

Quinn & Cameron (1988b) asked 12,000 employees of American companies what characterized an effective organization and effective managers. These employees were chosen because they worked for companies who had succeeded in creating a foundation of employee well-being. The employees' answers reflected some overall paradoxical demands to the organization, which span various sectors, sizes, and company cultures. The results were divided into two groups: those that showed a focus on internal dimensions and those that focused on external dimensions. The externally focused answers indicated that the company was successful due to its focus on surroundings, such as visions, strategies, and goal-fulfillment. The internally focused answers credited the company's success to internal factors such as teamwork, democratic decision-making, clear workflow and procedures, and a high level of well-being.

Quinn and Cameron also found that a successful company needed to be focused and stable, as well as flexible and ready for change. On the one hand, a company should always do what it is best at and, on the other hand, it should continuously change itself. Quinn and Cameron called this the *competing values* of a company. The essential element of their work was the fact that they observed that a company's paradoxical approach resulted in success. Groups of directors concerned themselves equally with a focus on internal and external elements. They also focused on both flexibility regarding developing people and markets and stability, or the question about how to define the company's workflow and goals.

For several years I have used this model in collaboration with groups of directors. It makes sense for the company directors to think about their leadership tasks as managing competing values. Although the competing values of the model only represent a few of the many organization paradoxes that exist, I have found it to be a useful tool when trying to discover a shared understanding of the relevant challenges that face a group of directors.

The Danish Defense Academy is one of the Danish organizations that has worked intensively with paradoxes as a part of the foundation for its leadership. This foundation was formulated in 2008, and contains demands for handling a variety of paradoxes, which are theoretically based on Quinn and Cameron's idea of competing values as well as various other theoretical influences. They have adjusted the concepts of Quinn and Cameron's model to fit their needs, and have called it Change, Stability, Relations, and Results. These terms are a better fit for Danish culture than Quinn and Cameron's original terms, just as they are better able to

54 Paradoxical leadership development

reflect the challenges faced by the Defense Academy. The content is nearly identical to Quinn and Cameron's concepts, but the Defense Academy chose concepts that reflect their everyday and organizational culture and values.

I have chosen to build on the Defense Academy's version of the Competing Values Framework model in order to describe the four elements of a company in relation to organizational paradoxes. I have used them in my consultant practice in both leadership development programs and educational settings, as well as in my foundation for developing organizations. I have found that this makes more sense than using the original concepts from the Competing Values Framework model.

The concepts which are used in the Danish Defense Academy's foundation for leadership are as follow:

> Externally flexible focus = Change
> Internal focus = Stability
> External focus = Results
> Internally flexible focus = Relationships

The model that I will use in this book, which is an integration of the Defense Academy's concepts and Quinn and Cameron's model is shown in Figure 4.1.

Organizational paradoxes

Flexible

Relations / Doing it together:
- Commitment, welfare
- Coordinated collaboration
- Learning, knowledge sharing
- Values and culture
- Empower team

Renewal / Being the first to do it:
- Following the market
- Positioning
- Visionary
- Product development
- Being creative

Internal — *External*

Stability / Doing correctly:
- Stability and safe service
- Documentation
- Systematic
- Guidelines and rules
- Quality control

Results / Doing quickly:
- Goal oriented
- Value for society and for the client
- Strategies for achievement of goals
- Competition

Focused

FIGURE 4.1 Competing Values Framework: organizational paradoxes

The following section will explore the model and provide a closer description of each of the quadrants. It starts with some general descriptions of what is in focus, then moves to a description of the theoretical foundation for each quadrant, and ends with a presentation of key words for the thought process that is behind the quadrant as well as the how change is viewed within the quadrant.

External and flexible: change

In order to follow the market and the needs of the customer/user/citizen, a company needs to change and develop accordingly. This is necessary in order to live up to ambient demands and needs, but also to be seen and heard as a visible player in the market. This is important in regard to products, markets, marketing, etc. To be in a state of change means that the company is good at anticipating tendencies, thinking of groundbreaking ideas, experimenting, and doing something that hasn't been seen before. In other words, it means thinking outside the box.

A metaphor for change is Barack Obama's "yes we can" policy. His policy was an entirely new way of tackling development. He achieved this by using a new way of understanding the role of government. Here is another example of this idea:

> The director group of a company that produces products for the construction industry had been discussing how they should market their product for a long time. They had contacted construction magazines, created advertisements, written articles in newspapers and magazines, and held arrangements within the field, all without results. Sales were not increasing. At a seminar, they began to be interested in other untried and nontraditional methods of coming in contact with customers.
>
> One of the employees in the marketing division said that he had a group of friends who were construction workers, and they had all said that they would be most likely to see an advertisement in *Ekstra Bladet* (a popular Danish tabloid magazine) rather than in a construction magazine.

This is an example of how the sales company moved into the change quadrant. They used an informed opinion to discover what might be effective, and thereby found a good idea for using a different type of marketing.

The key words for organizations with focus on change are: visions, interaction with surroundings, learning, network, interests, optimism, co-creation, innovative leadership, flexibility, entirety, future, curiosity, investigation, creativity, context-dependency (few to no finished concepts), and constant development.

External and focused: results

Result-oriented companies focus on what needs to happen in order for them to achieve their goals. They create a strategy and stick to it. This does not only mean that they outperform others in the market, but also that they are goal-oriented and ambitious regarding what it takes to succeed. Once they have an idea, create a strategy, or develop a vision, they are quick to achieve their goals and cross the finish line. Here is an example:

> A new director was hired in order to create results for an order and project-oriented company that had had problems with growth. In the course of the first week he had created a plan. The plan was that part of production should be moved out of the country, and that the company should cut down on the number of solutions they offered customers. This would allow the company to move away from large project solutions and toward smaller solutions. After the first week, the director stood on his soap-box, and announced these changes in short and precise speech. Although this meant that there would be lay-offs in some places in the organization, the employees knew that it was necessary. The director had created an urgency for them. The director's next step was to conduct individual interviews with each of the employees so that they understood what they should each achieve in order for their part of the plan to succeed. For example, he said, "We will implement this aggressive plan to avoid having to fire more people, but in order for it to succeed, the sales department needs to sell X amount of projects, and throughout the course of the year, X amount of production needs to be moved abroad. We need to have the best offer in regard to both price and quality of X."

As this example shows, a result-oriented company in the midst of a process of change is quick to make ongoing decisions that maximize value through project portfolios, to closely monitor individual employees (or managers), and to reward employees or teams that have high levels of performance. Being competitive can be described using these key words: efficiency, productivity, waste, customer-value, action, initiative, goals and resources, strategies, quick decisions, mile-posts, follow up, incentives, "winner-culture," governance, result-contracts, return on investment (ROI), market.

Internal and flexible: relationships

Focusing on internal elements within an organization means nurturing cooperation. This means that the external parameters are only successful if the organization is able to maintain focus on the people within the organization. Focusing on cooperation means the development of an organization that is able to learn, share knowledge internally, and work according to shared goals and values. This describes an organization that has adequate focus on cooperation and relationships, and believes that results are best created through well-being, involvement, unity, etc. In other words, the human elements are the most important factor in determining whether an organization is successful. Here is an example:

> A company in the supermarket branch wanted to work with a process of cultural change that would help them to increase their market shares. In the preliminary meeting, the director said, "We have a lot of focus on our product. People stay here for a long time. They are extremely loyal, and that is what has brought us to where we are today. We need to maintain this if we want to continue to grow. We need to develop a culture where employees have a high level of communications, where they feel that they have responsibility, and that they use each other in the optimal way. You could say that we have a family culture. We know what is going on in each other's lives, we support one another, take over for one another when we can't do things ourselves, and we know that the employees will make an extra effort if the need arises. The culture that we need to strengthen is an ownership-culture with a high degree of responsibility and team spirit."

The key phrase in the relationship-oriented quadrant is: "it's all about people." Key words that describe this quadrant are: people, potential motivation, synergy, communication, appreciation, development, cooperation, culture, unconscious and irrational behavior, personality, involvement, dialogue, education and training, values, team organizational development, consensus, conflict resolution, team-building, personal assessments, communication training, coaching.

Internal and focused: stability

Stability simply begins with a company focusing on creating stability in work-processes, and therefore in the way the organization performs. This is done through a focus on control and follow-up, which optimizes workflow, systems, agreements, employee resources, rules, frameworks, guidelines, and quality control. This ensures that "the machine" runs efficiently. There are many approaches to "tuning" the organization so that it can efficiently handle and solve multiple complex tasks, many people, and reoccurring problems/tasks. Here is an example:

> A smaller consultant company was undergoing rapid development, and was in danger of growing too fast. Tasks were multiplied, the number of employees rose from 12 to 76 in one year, the company found success in many countries and began to purchase other companies. The company implemented project-management systems, time registration (in order to streamline customer billing), personal manuals, and LEAN projects. As a result, as one of the employees said, "it is sometimes hard to find out if someone has dealt with the customer's inquiries, or if I need to call them back, because we're still working on getting a system working which will allow us to handle the growth. Something has to be stable in our daily workflow when so much else is changing all the time. Otherwise we can't orient ourselves in all the new things we have to relate to."

58 Paradoxical leadership development

People, potential, motivation, synergy, communication, appreciation, development, teamwork, culture, unconscious and irrational behavior, personality, involvement, dialogue, education and training, values, team, organizational development, consensus, conflict management

Visions, interaction with the surroundings, learning, networks, interests, optimism, co-creation, innovative leadership, flexibility, the whole, future, curiosity, investigation, creativity

Continuity, standardization, reliability, ensured delivery, specialization, systematization, distribution of responsibility and competences, information, control, rationality, functionality, analysis, details

Efficiency, productivity, waste, customer-value, action, initiative, goals and resources, strategies, quick decisions, mileposts, follow-up of results, incentives, "winner culture", management, result-based contracts, ROI, market

FIGURE 4.2 Competing paradigms

Source: Adapted in collaboration with Kuno Johansen (colleague) based on Cameron and Quinn (2005).

The key phrase for the stability-oriented organization is "machine room." The key words to describe this quadrant are: continuity, standardization, reliable operation, ensured delivery, specializing, systematization, distribution of responsibility and competence, information, control, rationality, functionality, analysis, details, quality-control, no errors, documentation, focus on the facts, classic project leadership, project planning, risk analysis.

To sum up, we have four approaches to organizational challenges that are in contrast with each other, but are at the same time closely connected. This is exactly what characterizes the paradox. The paradigm bridge is built between potential change/stability and cooperation/results. The quadrants are shown in Figure 4.2.

In Chapter 2, we saw how competing paradigms contributed to a complete understanding of managerial tasks. Figure 4.2 reflects these competing paradigms, in that the postmodern paradigm can be seen in the relationship and change paradigms. Tools that are used in these forms of leadership are: innovative leadership, creativity, leadership-based coaching, team development, dialog processes, recognition of communication tools, etc. The modern paradigm is reflected in the stability and results quadrants, which are characterized by project-management tools, goal-implementation tools, documentation, goal-management, etc. As we can see in the model, these paradigms are contained (and juxtaposed) as paradoxes, which the organization needs to successfully navigate. The model and competing values are standing on the "paradigm bridge" and are an integrative model in relation to the otherwise mutually exclusive paradigms. This should not be seen as a complete and universal model, and I do not claim that it is in any way an exhaustive representation of all the complex problems, ambiguities, and ambivalence that managers face. However, I have found the model to be a useful tool for coordinating shared leadership initiatives within a management team.

Summary

I often see a management team that works well together regarding questions of drive as well as discussions of strategy. However, in daily life, the management team should also meet in order to coordinate leadership effort and to discuss leadership as a discipline that supports the organization's goals and values. The Competing Values Framework model, which outlines the organizational paradoxes, is extremely useful when investigating the status of an organization, discussing which relevant challenges exist, and coordinating the initiatives of individual managers.

REFLECTIONS: USEFUL QUESTIONS FOR THE MANAGEMENT TEAM

1. If we look at the diagram of the organizational paradoxes, where does it seem our focus has been lately?
2. Where has that led the organization?
3. What kind of company culture is created by this focus?
4. How do we notice this culture?
5. Which strategy does the company need to succeed in the near future?
6. Keeping the company's vision/strategy in mind, where should we focus in order to succeed?

As we have seen in this chapter, organizational paradoxes require us to treat an organization as something that consists of contradictory values and demands. We could almost say that there is a centrifugal and centripetal force in the organization's life, and that we must take this into account and make an effort to balance the two forces. The contradictory values pull in opposite directions, which is a reality for every organization. The values must continually be balanced through leadership so that the organization can succeed and develop in a healthy balance.

If you want to work with company growth and development, you must relate to new goals and new thinking as well as stability and internal relations.

Organizational paradoxes are the foundation for strategic considerations and decisions. In order for management to avoid being driven by the individual manager's personality or ideas about what good leadership is, it is necessary to use organizational paradoxes to form the "arena" where you and your management team can navigate the complex organizational problems. In the next chapter, I will describe what the organizational paradoxes mean to the various types of leadership positions. We will examine how leadership is exercised, and which roles and positions can reflect competing values in practice.

5

ORGANIZATIONAL PARADOXES IN PRACTICE

Examples of organizational change

The Competing Values Framework resembles many familiar leadership models: Adizes, Belbin, Discover, situation-based leadership, etc. However, there is an especially appealing dimension to the paradox model in that it accounts for the fact that leadership must be organized according to the organizational needs of a given moment. Working with formulating the problems that arise due to a planned organizational change is a part of the leadership task.

Much of the leadership literature is concerned with how change is created. Kotter (in *Leading Change* (1996) and *The Heart of Change* (2002)) describes these processes, as well as how to plan in a way that includes change. Strategic literature can be used to create a framework in order to investigate what needs to be changed. The director/management group can use competing values as an impetus to determine the focus of the organization in order to achieve a chosen strategy (organizational paradoxes), and therefore decide which type of leadership action is required (role paradoxes).

In this chapter, we will examine how the Competing Values Framework (CVF) can be used in practice in order to implement organizational change. The chapter will provide examples of how the model has been used as a strategic tool in order to help change the growth of an organization. We will see how the model helped a management group work within the paradox between external and internal focus. It also helped them make the decision to increase internal focus with the goal of continuing toward their growth strategy.

Carletti: organizational strengths and managerial needs

Carletti is a Danish company that makes chocolate and candy for retail. It has 150 employees in Denmark. The brand is especially known for its "P-pies" (miniature chocolate-covered peanut and nougat pies) and marshmallow bananas (chocolate-covered, banana-flavored marshmallow). The company began as a family business and in 2006 it hired an experienced administrative director to help expand the company.

After five years of growth, Carletti became one of the minor players among the large companies in a very competitive market, and there was a desire to evaluate the culture that was developing within the company. The director wanted to increase employee development and help them to take more ownership. His goal was to prevent senior management from becoming a bottleneck, and to ensure that decisions could be made efficiently, non-centrally, and be implemented quickly. At the same time, management wanted to place more focus on making workflow more efficient as well as thoroughly considering new products. The company needed to move through the development process with both high speed *and* high precision. The director explained that the company had grown thanks to the fact that both employees and managers acted within an innovative, entrepreneurial culture with high levels of collaboration, loyalty, and a "we'll take it as it comes" and "we'll make an extra effort" mentality. He explained that the company's success was due to the idea that everyone helped each other, everyone worked loyally to make things work, and that management was closely connected to the values of the employees and company.

Management recognized that they had perhaps reached the limits of how far they could go with a focus on new products and fast results. It was time to provide clear definitions of work assignments and for management to use more time on approaches for development and strategy. This required that the company knew that they had created effective decision-making structures (stability) and that employees were autonomous and able to manage themselves (relationships).

Status of the organization with CVF as a tool

When I worked with management to help create development within the organization, our first approach was to identify how and where the company was moving. We found CVF to be a useful tool. If we analyze the situation using the model for organizational paradoxes, we can see that the director's description of the company's focus lies within the results and change quadrants. This means that the company had an external focus for both the relationships–results paradox and the change–stability paradox. Management had been innovative and the company had launched an extensive number of new products over a short period of time. The overall focus was external, and the company functioned because production, sales, and transportation followed demand.

This resulted in a good reputation and punctual deliveries. Sales increased and results were achieved in a short time. There was a lot of change (top-right in the model shown in Figure 5.1) and there was also a lot of focus on achieving goals and results. The management group was focused on what Quinn and Cameron called the "external/outward focus."

The company grew and as a result it had trouble maintaining a rhythm. Managers discussed the fact that it was hard to keep up with their own success. There was an

Organizational paradoxes

```
                        Flexible

          Relations                          Change
        Doing it together              Being the first to do it

         Commitment, welfare    │  Following the market
         Coordinated            │  Positioning
         collaboration          │  Visionary
         Learning, knowledge    │  Product development
         sharing                │  Being creative
         Values and culture     │
Internal Empower team           │                          External
         ───────────────────────┼───────────────────────
         Stability and safe     │  Goal oriented
         service                │  Value for society and for
         Documentation          │  the client
         Systematic             │  Strategies for achievement
         Guidelines and rules   │  of goals
         Quality control        │  Competition

          Stability                          Results
        Doing it correctly              Doing it quickly

                        Focused
```

FIGURE 5.1 Focus on the external polarities of the paradoxes

increasing need for an internal focus to supplement the external focus. Management realized that efficiency and external competition resulted in a need for more ownership, process-skills, and stable workflow.

Strategic development initiatives

The Carletti management group and I identified two key areas that needed our focus: stability and relationships. These two areas are the more internally focused areas in the CVF model. We examined these areas using the change–stability paradox and found that the company's ability to compete in the market could be strengthened by moving focus away from launching new products, original labels, alternative sales methods, and product development and instead focusing on describing how workflow should operate, procedures to correct mistakes, registration of new orders, creation of a customer database, and a description of new development. This change in focus was a 180-degree turn toward stability. This turn meant that the management group needed to increase and develop the part of their leadership that dealt with making sure agreements were followed, following up on procedures, taking personal responsibility for follow-up, and using management group meetings to ensure that everything was running smoothly.

The management group viewed this as a huge challenge and, as the director said, "we will need to have focus on stability without slowing down our pace, and we can't stop doing what has worked up to now in an effort to create stability." We discussed the fact that the challenge was to turn their backs on something in order to face something else for a while. Changing focus is often easier said than done, because management is often afraid that if they change their focus, the areas that have created results will not function as well. They feel that it can be compared to having to shift gears and lose speed right when you are about to pass someone in a race. It is often a fear of short-term consequences that prevents management from shifting focus toward the part of the paradox they have previously avoided. This is clearly reflected in statements such as:

> We can't lose speed while we figure out the internal guidelines

and

> This shouldn't be understood as meaning that we should stop being there when things need to be delivered on time

or

> We can't believe that a company like ours can be sustained through just focusing on a strategic task. We will still have to be there with the employees if there is a problem in order to make sure that they keep up the pace.

All of these statements were true enough, but the action that followed needed to change.

When a company needs to change focus, it is a completely normal reaction for them to not want to "release the accelerator to change gears." The majority agree with the fact that it will be necessary in the long run, but it feels unnatural for a company to ease up on the elements that have been successful so far.

However, in this phase of the change process, management must recognize that a stable platform is necessary for the long-term growth strategy to succeed. If management only thinks in terms of change and concrete performance goals, they risk only going as far as the organization's current situation allows. In the Carletti example, there was a need for management to look internally in order to move forward by re-examining and renewing product launches, customer relations, documentation, procedural descriptions, etc. Therefore, I found that the management group recognized both the need to shift focus as well as the risks associated with doing so.

The other parameter that Carletti management needed to focus on was a movement away from *results* and towards a *relationship*-oriented focus. The management group wanted to be able to increase focus on meeting and developing the longer-term goals and visions of the company. However, this meant that the employees and middle management had to increase their sense of ownership and teamwork. One of the results was that all employees had to agree on where the company was going, have the opportunity to receive necessary help from their closest manager, and feel involved in the company's operations. This would result in the employees being able to work together to fix mistakes, discuss how tasks should be solved, and have a feeling that the ability to solve problems was dependent on different competences within a diverse team.

In order to help employees reach these goals, management created an educational program for middle managers with the goal of making paradoxical thinking beneficial for all managers, and to help middle management support and involve employees to develop a higher degree of ownership around shared problem-solving. As an employee stated,

> it is important that employees in this company can see a connection and a reason for what they have to do – that they feel like we pull together, need each other, and work well together. There are a lot of assignments where you are dependent on each other, so it is important that we have a well-functioning team we can rely on and succeed with. The worst that could happen when things are moving quickly is that we let go of the individual, and then it becomes meaningless to work so hard if we don't feel that we are a community working together. It's even worse if an employee doesn't fully understand why you once in a while need to make an extra effort, and that it won't work if others don't do the same.

Therefore, the company needs to ensure that the human element of growth will thrive through creating good teamwork, a high degree of involvement and feeling of community, and individual ownership. It is important that management makes sure that results are not achieved at the cost of well-being and cooperation, because in the end this will negatively affect results. Therefore, the Carletti management group needed to focus on its members and their role in creating motivation, well-being, cooperation, and shared responsibility for each other and their assignments.

The movement we started is illustrated in Figure 5.2.

This example shows how a concrete process of change can start from a shared understanding of the movement that is needed. Throughout the process, the following thoughts were shared:

> We have to re-fuel so that we have fuel – *and* we have to re-fuel in the air…
> We can't forget that our current leadership approach has actually brought us to this point, so…
> We need to develop the employees – *and* we can't lose our momentum.
> The director group needs to focus more on the big picture – *and* ensure that middle-management can keep things running smoothly.
> We need to know what is going on in the organization (ensure results) – *and* we need to support the initiatives of the employees, even if it isn't exactly what we would have done.

66 Paradoxical leadership development

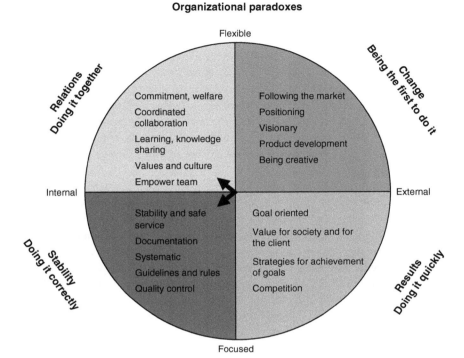

FIGURE 5.2 Movement toward the internal poles in the paradox

We need to have some patience – *and* we don't have enough time to create change.

There was a feeling of insecurity in changing the current leadership focus that had been the driving force behind the organization's success. The paradox consisted of the fact that they knew that something had to change, and at the same time they also wanted to ensure the success they had experienced so far.

The Carletti example, just like the Lego example, shows how the organizational paradox between stability and change was experienced as an urgent situation. Both companies handled this paradox by having the courage to take the step that would ensure the next organizational boost. This first step meant that the companies needed to make managerial changes toward a more internal focus and therefore strengthen the externally focused activities. Results would be further strengthened through relationships, just as change would happen through the creation of a more stable foundation (workflow, procedures, systems, etc.).

The Carletti example shows how CVF can function as a tool to talk about which leadership focus an organization should have, based on what the organization wants to achieve. The model combines strategy with leadership focus. The Carletti management group could therefore use the model to discuss what switching from an external to an internal focus meant for their leadership practice.

The model can be used as a basis for discussing which focus is needed to succeed, and which focus a management group needs to have in order to implement the desired organizational change. The organizational paradoxes do not say anything about how the managers should act, but rather what their focus should be. Therefore, the CVF model can be used as a basis for creating a shared understanding of the contradictory demands faced by the management group. This allows the managers to be able to share the challenges that underlie a difficult shift in focus.

Summary

As we will see later in the book, we can see organizational paradoxes, role paradoxes, and sense-of-belonging paradoxes in the Carletti example, but the bulk of the work was with the organizational paradoxes as a basis for change.

Organizational paradoxes describe the fundamental contradictory values that arise in processes of change within every organization, but they don't provide an immediate answer to the question of how managers should act. Organizational paradoxes are also relevant for how we can understand leadership roles in all of their complexity.

REFLECTION: ORGANIZATIONAL PARADOXES

1. What are the relevant processes of change within your organization?
2. How does this affect the employees?
3. Where are the employees looking for clarity?
4. How do you provide this clarity?
5. Does your communication include complexity, or do you avoid ambiguity when speaking to your employees?
6. How can you talk to your managers and employees about the fact that paradoxes are a necessary part of the processes of change?

In the next chapter, we will examine the contradictory demands made on managers during a paradoxical process of change. We will also see how CVF can also be used as a conceptual apparatus for a leadership practice that matches the contradictory demands of the organization.

6

THE ROLE PARADOX

Contradictory demands of leadership

As I showed earlier in the book, working with Lego allowed me to conclude that there are three levels of paradoxes: the organizational level, where I identified a number of fundamental organizational paradoxes, the leadership level, also called role paradoxes, and the emotional level, or sense-of-belonging paradoxes.

In Chapters 4 and 5, I described how managers and management teams can relate to organizational paradoxes. Through these descriptions, it became clear that it is advantageous for managers to relate to organizational paradoxes, especially when a company is in the process of change. My claim is that organizational paradoxes are a necessary condition of the organization. For example, there will always be tension between stability and change, just as there is a contradictory relationship between people and profit, and these tensions need to be balanced in any organization. Both efficiency and well-being can be created within a company if the manager understands how to use these paradoxes to lead, without turning away from any of the alternatives.

In the previous chapter, I explained organizational paradoxes with the help of the theory of competing values. In this chapter, I will examine role paradoxes, which describe the function and behavior that is expected of management/the individual manager. I have found that the CVF model is a useful framework to use when working with management groups and boards of directors. It provides a way to understand and discuss leadership while working to create a shared picture of what kinds of leadership action are needed in the organization.

The fact that we can depict organizational life as a set of paradoxes has a large impact on how managers should practice their personal leadership. This is also reflected in the more personal paradoxes of competing roles. For example, a manager has different roles depending on whether he or she is working to create an effective team, or if he or she is working to increase the team's performance and provide new demands and goals.

While organizational paradoxes give rise to answers to the strategic question "What does the organization need to accomplish in the future?", role paradoxes revolve around the more practical question, "What should I, as a manager, focus on in the future in order to implement the strategy?"

Role paradoxes in Lego

Lego's 11 leadership paradoxes are examples of role paradoxes. They describe what is required of managers, as well as the concrete roles managers have in relation to the employees and the organization. Therefore, they directly describe how leadership should unfold.

> As managers, we are usually the ones who can do everything ourselves. You are expected to have all the answers, be the best technician, and be confident. We are usually promoted because of our ability to go first, but now we have to do something else. We have to be more people-oriented, but still focused on the products. And we are expected to show our insecurities and still be authority figures. It is hard to understand all of that!

The role of the Lego managers changed due to the changes in the organization's tasks and structure. As the above quote illustrates, the implementation of an autonomous team had a profound effect on the leadership role. It became difficult for the manager to understand what it meant to be the manager of a team that was autonomous, and it wasn't immediately apparent what that meant in relation to the new leadership roles. Examples of new questions the manager had were: "What is a good leadership performance in this new organization?" and "How should managers understand themselves as leaders, if their previous leadership roles are no longer valued?"

The managers felt that it was crucial to create a meaningful leadership role in relation to their production team. They did not feel comfortable balancing authority and a high degree of employee involvement. How could they be responsible authority figures and still allow others to make their own decisions? How could they focus and motivate employees when they were also under pressure to increase production?

In other words, the Lego managers were challenged on a personal level. Their experience was one of feeling torn in half and being in a dilemma that couldn't be solved. Whenever they tried to define the new role, they found a contradiction in their assigned task. Here is an example where one manager tried to create meaning out of the apparent contradiction of both going first and staying behind as a manager:

> "If I wanted the members of the production team to cooperate better, maybe I should speak with them individually. But that would go against the idea that they should be autonomous. Is their conflict – which impairs efficiency and well-being – their problem, or is it mine?"

The manager was confronted by that part of the managerial role that he didn't account for when trying to find an unambiguous role. Later in the conversation he said:

"Maybe you are right, they should be more responsible for solving their own problems. But will they do it? And what if they don't? I am still responsible for the efficiency of the team. So I can't just let them tackle it on their own."

The manager had now re-thought his dilemma and was in danger of moving in the opposite direction. He was now thinking about staying in the background and letting the team members solve the problem themselves. However, as in many other examples from Lego, it turned out that the complexity of the problem prevented the manager from using his accustomed unambiguous and linear thinking.

Why did the manager's roles become so complex and ambiguous? Linda Putnam (1986), who has worked extensively with organizational communication, claims that conflicting and ambiguous roles in connection with organizational change are the result of interpersonal communication between managers and their employees. The paradox is generated as a part of the information and messages that are provided at various levels within the organization. For example, a senior manager tells his employees that he has confidence in the fact that they can run the company while he is gone and yet he constantly calls to check up on them. He is in danger of sending contradictory signals to his employees. His words say, "I trust you," while his actions say, "I don't trust you." As Putnam states, the manager might be unaware that he is sending conflicting signals, but his employees still have to interpret both types of signals. Of course, the reaction of the employees is important, but the manager's signals can easily create confusion.

Another example can be seen in the way that Danish elementary schools are in the midst of a large organizational paradox. The schools must now keep difficult students in the classroom, but at the same time they must increase the academic level of teaching. The role of the school's principal is to support the employees and help them to focus on academic initiatives, while simultaneously challenging them to include children with special needs. They need to navigate the role paradox between support and challenge.

Table 6.1 shows a number of the role paradoxes that the Lego managers worked with.

Role paradoxes are the category of paradoxes that come closest to answering the question "What is most useful for me/we to do (as manager/management team) right now in relation to the (paradoxical!) strategy of the company?"

As could be expected, there is no simple answer to this question, but there are some tools that can be used to continuously identify management's paradoxical roles in relation to the relevant organization challenges. However, role paradoxes require a reflective distance, which means that management needs to take a position

TABLE 6.1 Role paradoxes

The problem →	The dilemma →	The paradox →	→ Toward workable certainty
Involve your employees/Increase production.	Should I spend time involving the employees **or** should I just make sure that they increase production?	Involvement takes time **and** involving employees saves time.	I will make a plan for activities that involve employees and have the goal of increasing productivity.
If my team should be autonomous, what is my role?	Should I lead them **or** should I let them run the business themselves?	Bottom-up **and** top-down leadership.	I will make sure that my team always has enough clarity, direction, and insight to be able to lead and delegate themselves. I will see them as a whole, but they must relate to each other on their own.
How do I avoid conflicts so that the employees can work efficiently and well together?	Should I handle the conflict **or** should I insist that they solve it?	Release creativity and focus on getting things under control.	Work with the conflict and help them to release their creativity and work together.
How can I motivate people when they are so different?	Should I focus on the differences **or** should I treat them all the same?	Create unity **and** focus on difference.	I will have to treat people differently and make different demands of them if I want to create a homogeneous group.
How do I stay in the background when I know the best way to solve problems?	Should I let them find the solution themselves **or** should I give them the solution because that is faster?	Go ahead **and** stay in the background.	I will need to allow them to know my thoughts about the solution so that they can use that in their deliberations about how they will solve the problem in their own way.

on which role is useful at any given moment with regard to the relevant strategies and needs of the organization.

CVF and personal leadership

When we discuss personal leadership, I am not referring to the individual manager's psychological background, personality, etc., but to the behavior that each manager must demonstrate in order to implement the strategic focus of the organization.

If we use CVF to explain personal leadership, we find that personal leadership means the practical implementation of organizational paradoxes. This requires managers to be able to have many different roles. We can see that organizational paradoxes are reflected in the manager's role paradoxes. If the manager of a management group needs to manage a process of change where focus moves from change to stability, he or she will have to change roles from a visionary/investigative role to a more practical/maintenance role with the intention of creating increased stability.

The following section describes two leadership roles within each of the organization's quadrants in the CVF model. This can be useful when organizing leadership action. These role paradoxes should not be understood as complete descriptions of the leadership positions that can be found in organizations, but simply as one framework that can help create a shared understanding of what is needed and which roles can be advantageous in order to successfully create organizational change. The model is shown in Figure 6.1.

In the following sections, I will describe the paradoxical roles that are connected to the organizational paradoxes of "change–stability" and "results–relationships."

Manager roles between change and stability

Change means that you, as a manager, need to be able to be a visionary, develop new ways of doing things, and create an image of where the company or department is headed. It means thinking creatively and finding the company's next step. This could be, for example, changing the company's presence in the market or improving performance.

In a radio presentation from April 15, 2010, the management researcher Anne Mette Digmann explained that almost all managers state that their most important task is to create space and a framework for their employees to use to solve problems. This statement is sharply contrasted by the employees' answer: they most often believe that their managers' most important task is to be a strategic visionary.

The difference between the answers of the managers and employees could be explained by the fact that the employees experience managers who take over and organize the employee tasks, and therefore the employees do not feel that they lack a framework. Perhaps the answer would have been different if the manager only focused on vision and strategy, without having a sense for the employees' tasks and supporting them. Regardless, the research shows that employees value visionary development from managers. The change quadrant shows these roles.

Role paradox **73**

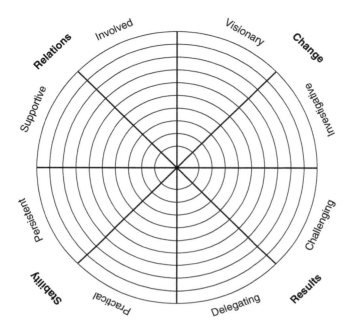

FIGURE 6.1 The wheel of leadership roles

A manager who is good at creating change within a company (being a visionary) will most often be seen as a person who is good at floating new ideas. This type of manager is always looking for good ideas and new ways to accomplish tasks, as well as new business areas, new angles of attack, new products, etc. A manager with focus on development is good at multitasking and often exudes energy and innovative thinking.

In other words, the role of a leader is to represent two overall disciplines:

1. **Be visionary**, develop new visions and scenarios and help people follow them.
2. **Be investigative**, use internal and external networks, and have a curious and investigative approach.

A manager should also be able to see opportunities, quickly adjust to changes, accurately read a situation, and provide flexible organization. This means that a manager needs to be good at communicating visions and inspiring others to see and follow the potential new perspectives. An innovative and flexible culture is best achieved by using the following elements:

> Continual – and potentially radical – adjustments
> External contacts and networks
> Vision

74 Paradoxical leadership development

> Creativity
> Problem-solving
> Responsiveness to "the new"
> Resourcefulness

Therefore, it is important that managers are engaged with developing and communicating visions so that employees have something to be passionate about and work towards achieving. The areas of focus are transformative leadership, vision, creative problem-solving, willingness to take risks, and diversity.

It has been shown that successful companies have an openness and investigative attitude toward their surroundings, product-development, work forms, etc.

Managers who lead by being investigative are, according to Dyer and his colleagues (2011), more successful at creating organizations that are good at changing themselves. There are five elements that describe the investigative manager:

- Associate with what you hear and experience, think about how you can be inspired, and collaborate with others to develop and adjust ideas.
- Ask questions – of everything you see and hear – both internally and externally.
- Observe – keep an eye out for who is working on something/thinking about something that looks interesting.
- Experiment – reward innovative employee behavior.
- Network – be open to everything that could be beneficial to change.

It is important to note that not all managers are naturally inclined to take on the visionary or investigative position in the organization. If you want to improve your role as a strategic visionary, there are areas such as innovation-leadership, network-leadership, creative thinking, the Blue-Ocean strategy, etc. that are available to you. These areas can provide tools to strengthen your own leadership role as a visionary and investigative strategist.

The other half of the change–stability paradox is stability. Stability means making sure that the "machine" runs as it should. Although employees in the public sector claim that managers must first and foremost be strategic visionaries, there is also an unspoken need for projects to be finished, and for the manager to maintain functional workflow, work procedures, tools for documentation, IT systems, etc. In addition to ensuring that the practical elements run smoothly, the stability role deals with maintaining goals and strategies as well as keeping employees focused and loyal to the organization's goals.

The figures in Chapter 4 showed how the various quadrants had corresponding areas of focus. We used the metaphor of "a machine room" for the stability quadrant. The manager uses his or her professional (not necessarily expert) insights to know what is going on in the department/company. This work-form requires logic, realism, maintenance, and rational thinking. Stability is created through procedures and work-routines that ensure that everything runs efficiently. Systems and stable workflow are key issues. The organization's mantra is to do everything "better, cheaper, and safer." Predictability and stability are on the agenda.

In the stability quadrant, efficiency is best increased through action that focuses on stability and continuity. Clear hierarchies and delegation create a well-run organization where everything functions smoothly. Stability and continuity are achieved through:

> Rules/guidelines
> Stability in the organization
> Perseverance
> Focus on the details
> Schedules, structure

The role of a manager is to be practically oriented, find solutions to concrete task-related problems, design and coordinate as well as demonstrate confidence, and analyze and evaluate how well the "machine" (the organization) is running.

The types of behavior that support the stabilizing element in the company are:

- **Practical behavior**, where the manager brainstorms with employees and follows up to make sure that workflow, IT, and tasks are running efficiently.
- **Perseverance** regarding the implementation of visions, strategies, and practical problem-solving.

The level of the manager's skills in the stabilizing quadrant can vary. If you want to improve your abilities within this field you can participate in educational programs such as planning tools, LEAN, documentation tools, IT systems, etc. You can then ensure that your company or department functions as it should.

Both alternatives in the role paradox should be implemented. The paradoxical element of the leadership role is that you must be a visionary *and* be practical as well as being both investigative *and* persistent. Let's examine these roles more closely. First, I will describe the role on one end of the paradox, followed by some reflections that can be used to determine when and where this part of the role paradox should be prioritized. I will then describe the other end of the paradox. This may not immediately appear as the paradox that has been described, but in a later chapter I will return to how both alternatives can be implemented simultaneously. It is this simultaneity that makes many roles paradoxical: they are mutually contradictory while simultaneously relying on each other.

The role paradox: visionary–practical

Visionary behavior

Visionary behavior means that you have the role of being the one who orients employees, creates development, and contributes to change within the organization.

It requires you to not be buried in operational tasks, but to keep all possibilities open. This means that you need to be able to orient yourself in the world on behalf of the organization, and use the information and impressions from your surroundings to create development within your company/department.

First, the vision must be formulated in a way that it contains some sort of movement – there has to be something that everyone is working toward. Second, there needs to be an element that directs action. This will identify the direction that the organization should move toward. Third, the manager must ensure that there is connection to the vision. This is most easily done if the connection is personally meaningful for the manager. He or she must then create a meaningful momentum, which can be done through providing a detailed explanation of the vision for the employees. It is important that each employee can clearly see the vision and understand how they can connect to it.

The way in which the manager communicates regarding the vision is essential. The manager must stand up on his or her "soapbox." In order to communicate vision, employees must feel loyalty, duty, meaning, and a sense of the fighting spirit. In order to create these feelings among employees, managers must remember the following elements:

> Create, formulate, and develop a vision that will appeal to the community
> Communicate regarding the vision strategically, tactically, and personally in a way that allows each individual to relate to the vision
> Find a personal viewpoint and opinion regarding the vision, and act in a way that reflects this.

REFLECTION

1. To what degree do you contribute to innovation and development in your company?
2. How great is the need for innovation in your organization right now?
3. What types of work methods do you have in meetings with your employees? How do you stimulate innovation in the meetings?
4. How much effort do you make in formulating and presenting a clear vision – also throughout your daily routine?

Practical behavior

Practical orientation covers the manager's ability to create good, realistic planning and organization. A significant part of leadership is to create clarity regarding tasks, roles, and expectations. Although the manager must be focused on creating stability and continuity, he or she must still expect periodic changes, and realize that the organization needs both stability and development. However, even in the middle of change, there is a need for managers to focus on creating clarity regarding what needs to be done, and how to create stable workflow among the employees. In order to create this clarity, managers must focus on the following elements:

> Create clear work descriptions
> Communicate regarding expectations of employee roles and problem-solving
> Ensure that diverse projects are under control
> Prioritize between various activities
> Find tools that can ensure the daily operation of the department/company
> Coordinate and organize in relation to other departments and activities

To summarize, we can say that in this case, stability in the company is not about controlling whether or not employees do their jobs properly, but maintaining oversight and providing calm and stability. This ensures that the employees reliably work toward the agreed plans. In other words, stability is about defining the work that must be done, ensuring that employees collaborate to create clarity, and smoothing out the workflow, systems, and structures that support the functionality of the organization.

REFLECTION

1. How do you show your employees the importance of systems and structure?
2. Do you follow the implementation of new systems, workflow and structure through to completion?
3. How high do you value the practical and administrative employees?
4. Do you follow up on budgets, finances, etc.?
5. How much time do you spend coordinating and analyzing the tasks that must be completed?
6. How much do you prioritize finishing projects that have already started before new projects arise and demand attention?

It is up to the management group to determine priorities within leadership action. What is prioritized is dependent on which strategic focus is being used. It is obvious that there must be a balance between the two ends of the paradox. The above questions can help to provide reflection on where your leadership focus lies, to analyze your efforts, and evaluate whether adjustments need to be made.

In addition, there is another paradox that can be relevant to working with living up to the double demands of change and stability. This paradox will be discussed in the next section.

The role paradox "investigative–persistent"

Investigative behavior

In the book, *The Innovator's DNA* (2011), Jeff Dyer and his colleagues researched five central qualities of the 25 most innovative managers in the world. These managers were characterized using the following top-five skills: observing, questioning, experimenting, networking, and associating. This research fits well with the investigative behavior in our leadership role model. To be investigative means that the manager listens to and is open to new ideas, suggestions, and what he or she sees and hears. The manager needs to be good at assimilating these elements and working with them as well as maintaining flexibility regarding the organization. Openness and humility regarding others' input is a must.

Managers who want to demonstrate investigative behavior must be able to implement the following elements:

> Either spend time outside of the organization or send employees outside of the organization in order to have contact with the outside world – network
> Challenge employees to challenge habits as well as taken for granted solutions
> Occasionally reward crazy ideas (and mistakes) that are experimental
> Be prepared to take responsibility for large organizational changes if they are smarter/better ways to do things
> Maintain flexibility and a learning-rich environment among employees – praise adaptable employees

---

REFLECTION

1. To what extent is there a need for change within your organization right now?
2. To what degree do you investigate outside of the company in order to be inspired by new approaches?
3. To what degree do you create an innovative and creative environment in the company/your department?
4. How do you use your networks?
5. How do you incorporate employees' and colleagues' ideas into new approaches?

All leadership roles have a downside. When I am working with companies, I often hear employees complain about managers who have increased innovation and change in the form of good ideas, inspiration, etc. so much that the employees have completely lost their sense of direction. In the companies I work with, I hear that the employees thrive best when the manager isn't there so often. This is explained by employees who say: "then he doesn't get so many new ideas that we will have to add on to our already large workload. He is good at getting things started, but not at getting them finished." This shows that it is important for managers to be aware of the other side of this role paradox: perseverance.

Persistent behavior

Persistent behavior is needed in situations where the surroundings create insecurity, ambiguity, and ambivalence. In these situations is it important that the manager can cut through the confusion, provide direction, and maintain the organization's action plan. Implementation is the key word. A note to those managers who love creating change in their organization: persistent behavior is just as important in order to implement ideas.

Persistent behavior is a part of the stability quadrant and indicates a focus on the following elements:

1. Think about what needs to be thought through before something new is presented. How does this fit with what already exists? (So that people aren't presented with too many castles in the air.)
2. Ask people to bring good arguments when advocating for a change.
3. Be tolerant of the fact that conflicts or dissatisfaction can arise at times, but stick with what you think is best.

Persistent behavior means maintaining the organization's goals, even when they are challenged by the competition, managers'/employees' good ideas, economic trends, decrease in interest rates, or whatever else might disrupt the organization. Persistent behavior means that managers:

> Use facts and common sense in their arguments and justify their/the organization's decisions.
> Are well-prepared so that what they do and say is well-thought out and makes sense to the employees
> Attempt to be as reliable and predictable as possible
> Stick to what usually works, even if it is questioned, and therefore:
> Help to create security, predictability, and oversight among the personnel. This can be done by checking that action plans and agreements are followed, etc.

We have now seen the role paradoxes that reflect the organizational paradoxes between change and stability. I have described the two leadership paradoxes that the leadership role needs to balance (visionary–practical and investigative–persistent). We have seen that both parts are necessary. It is not a matter of everything having a time and place, but also of what assumptions are involved. Therefore, even though you can be forced to turn away from one dimension for a while because you have to focus on the other dimension, you can't do this for very long. For example, you simply cannot succeed in creating change if there isn't a stable foundation to support the changes. If everything is changing, there will be chaos and disruption. However, if there is only stability you will create stagnation, and the company won't be able to compete in the market, or your department won't be able to follow the rest of the company. In practice, you can only focus on one thing at a time, but you need to be able to account for both ends of the role paradox in your understanding of what is needed to succeed.

In the following section we will explore the leadership roles that reflect the other organizational paradox: the role paradox between results and relationships.

Leadership roles between results and relationships

In order to ensure efficiency and measurable results, managers must take on the leadership role that matches the organizational need for efficiency. It is important to stress that results aren't only relevant to organizations that focus on the bottom line, but also to the attitude that needs to be in the organization in order for it to succeed in achieving its goals. Results are also essential to ensure that projects are related to the company's core values and that the company is able to live up to the goals set by customers, citizens, or the board of directors. If, for example, a manager is unable to make economic cut backs or set new goals during decreased economic trends, depleted markets, etc., the company risks being unable to compete. In the same way, public institutions that don't make themselves visible to partners and customers, and that can't produce expected results, are at risk of being closed, merged, or outcompeted. Therefore, the competitive attitude that is connected with the results quadrant is important, even if we are talking about an organization in the care industry. We have seen examples from psychiatry where there are new private psychiatric offers and therefore a competition for "the customer's" favor, which determines who attracts the most customers. This places demands on the employees to "sell" their performance when they are in contact with the municipality and ensure that they can live up to the demands that have been made by the citizens and municipality.

Managers who focus on results are usually good at pushing employees forward and being the first to come forward with results. These managers are good at creating a sense of urgency so that the employees feel that it is necessary to work quickly to achieve results. The manager rewards result-oriented employees and believes that it isn't necessary to have all the details finished, as long as things are moving along.

The basic assumption of this focus area is that clear goals and ambition lead to productive results. Therefore, the leadership focus will be on making goals clear, making a logical and rational analysis, and encouraging action.

The manager's role will be to:

1. **Encourage**: Continually question whether employees/managers can do more/go farther and create increased efficiency in the organization. If a new policy isn't implemented, be critical in regard to what can be done.

2. **Delegate**: Create a sense of urgency and clarity regarding guidelines and expectations of the employees' performance. This means delegating tasks to both individuals and teams.

If you want to develop the aspects of the leadership role that focus on results, you can attend training for project management, goal management, result performance, LEAN six sigma, winner cultures, and sales communication (this is mostly to be able to give short and precise information to employees).

The efficiency of the manager is related to the company's productivity and profit/results. A competition-oriented culture is best created through implementing the following elements:

> Clear and ambitious goals
> Analysis of the situation
> Observance of action plans
> Rewarding action-oriented employees
> Creation of a sense of urgency
> Following up on the prescribed goals for teams and individuals

As we saw in the chapters about organizational paradoxes, results are connected to a manager's understanding of how to create a team and good relationships with the employees. This creates enthusiasm and ensures involvement.

Relationships are on the other side of results. The leadership of relationships is about having an internal focus as well as being oriented toward helping "the team play well together." Relationship orientation is about knowing what is needed for the employees to thrive both individually and collectively. Managers need to be both person- and group-oriented. There is a need for leadership tools such as patience, a listening approach, empathy, sensitivity, and for the manager to believe in the organization's values. The relationship-oriented leadership role focuses on giving employees space, allowing them to find their own way, and supporting them in what they want. This will create an organization where people do their best and work together. Relationships are important for the employees to feel that they want to create something together. The employees need to know that managers want the best for them, as well as knowing where they stand in relation to others.

When I work with organizations in order to increase their social capital, I can see that there has been a shift in content in the last few years. Social capital used to be about concepts such as confidence, justice, and cooperation. Now there is an increasing focus on the task at hand and creating results together. Social capital is about creating good relationships through problem-solving and good relationships improve problem-solving. Jody Gittell (2005), who has researched social capital in hospitals and airlines, claims that an understanding of the task at hand, the value of one's contribution to the whole, and how the collaboration can function creates high social capital. The coordination of relationships creates well-being and effectiveness.

In other words, managers must be concerned with the well-being of the team and the cooperative approach. A team-oriented culture is best achieved by encouraging the following elements among employees:

> Commitment/engagement
> Team spirit
> Community
> Motivation
> Synergy
> Shared understanding of how the individual contributes to the whole

The fundamental assumption is that a higher degree of involvement increases engagement, which increases the efficiency of problem-solving. Therefore, managers will need to focus on participation, employee development, conflict resolution, consensus, and creating a well-functioning team.

In order to strengthen the employees' feelings of community and ownership of the problem-solving process, the leadership role must:

1. **Be supportive.** Be present for the employees – listen to them.
2. **Involve employees.** In other words, be a facilitator with the goal of bringing the team together and creating a good team spirit where people feel engaged in their task and understand how they contribute to the larger shared tasks.

Not everyone feels comfortable working with relationships. If you are a manager who has been promoted because of your professional performance and you do not feel as confident about the human relationship aspects on the agenda, you may benefit from training in coaching, team-building, team development and communication, and organizational psychology. The relationships quadrant is the quadrant that is least directed toward work tasks. However, most employees and teams need a manager who can navigate this quadrant. A well-functioning team is one of the preconditions for the successful completion of a task.

When we frame the result–relationships quadrant as opposite leadership roles, we can see that managers must be able to navigate two paradoxical demands in order to succeed: involve *and* delegate as well as support *and* challenge employees.

Role paradox "supportive–challenging"

Supportive behavior

Supportive behavior means that the manager:

> Demonstrates concern when employees involve the manager in personal or difficult elements that have an impact on work
> Uses empathy to understand things from the employees' point of view – listen to what they are saying and understand the underlying message

> Is supportive, shows recognition for and pays attention to individual/team successes
> Ensures that each employee meets his or her potential. Use individual conversations and other forums in order to provide employees with the best possible opportunities to meet their potential. For teams: use team developmental conversations and follow up in relation to teamwork problems and team relationships
> Supports the development of the team's professional skills and group dynamics with the intention of optimizing teamwork.

Supportive behavior means that the manager shows interest in, and supports, the challenges facing employees and teams. The manager is also responsible for maintaining a good atmosphere and sense of well-being at work so that employees will want to improve, both individually and in collaboration with others.

REFLECTION

1. How well do you understand your own and others' motivation?
2. How do you work with employee and team development?
3. How do you show your employees that you see and hear them when they have a problem?
4. To what degree do you organize your meetings with the intention of providing employees with the opportunity to bring forward professional problems?

The advantage of placing relationships and well-being on the agenda is that you will be able to have a better understanding of where your employees are. Through working with relationships, you can gain a feeling for how much they can perform, how ambitious they are, how mature they are in reaction to solving problems, and how autonomous they are.

However, if you only focus on the relationship aspects of leadership, you will have employees who are happy and are good at discussing how their team functions, but who perhaps don't have such effective individual performance. The other end of the role paradox is challenging behavior, which requires a different work-form.

Challenging behavior

If a manager has a department or a team that needs more challenge and competition, he or she should work on creating clarity regarding goals, meaning, and expectations for employees. The manager needs to be good at creating goals, planning, being decisive, being inspiring, defining roles and tasks, creating guidelines, and giving instructions when needed.

There are several central questions that are connected to reflection on how a manager can best challenge his or her employees. These questions are relevant for the individual manager as well as the management team when providing a leadership focus in order to challenge the organization.

> **REFLECTION**
>
> 1. What does my part of the organization need to achieve? (goal)
> 2. How do we formulate SMART goals?
> 3. How do we create the appropriate incentives?
> 4. How do we best motivate the employees to reach the goals of the organization?

The first two questions should be answered based on the market or surroundings. What can we contribute to our surroundings, and therefore what should be our primary task? This then requires research into what the organization needs to do in order to reach the goal. The employees should also know this information, but the bulk of the answers to these questions will be provided from the external environment.

The third question asks how the organization will respond to these demands and how the organization can adapt to meet the goals. Employees can be involved in this stage, but the manager needs to have his or her own ideas about how this can be done.

It is almost like a team sport: it's about reading the surroundings and the challenges that are presented, sharing with the employees, creating the right team, and helping the employees understand the strategy and action plan. The manager should stand outside of the organization and examine it with a critical eye.

In the challenging leadership role, managers need to communicate their vision and provide concrete goals for their teams. It is important that the goals are realistic and measurable so that the employees know when they have succeeded. The manager should specify the direction in which the company should move, and ensure that there is a connection to the vision. This is most easily achieved if the vision and goal are meaningful to the manager. The manager can create a meaningful momentum by explaining the vision in detail to the employees. It is important that they are able to relate to the vision.

The manager must provide goals that are easily measured. One tool that can be useful here is the SMART model. The SMART model provides goals that are specific, measurable, ambitious, realistic, and time-dependent. The manager must also help the individual employee to make his or her effort visible. It is here that the manager can use a variety of goal-management tools, documentation tools, key performance indicators, etc. It is important that the employees know which goals they need to achieve and that the manager will follow up on their progress.

Challenging behavior most often is seen when the manager designs, organizes, and maintains effective guidelines. The manager has a focus on strategy. This is accomplished through the following points:

> How should the employees structure themselves so that they can best achieve the goal?
> Which "team position" should be created, and who has authority, competences, etc.?
> Use information and decision-making processes, structured meetings, meeting procedures, etc.
> Reward employees.
> Pay attention to people: who should have which position? Who needs additional support/challenge?

The role paradox between being supportive and challenging is often experienced by managers who feel that they have to be popular and unpopular at the same time. If you have a tendency to be friendly with your employees, it could be difficult to show authority and make demands on people. The postmodern paradigm, which is exemplified through supportive behavior, provides for an emotional connection between you and your employees. On the other hand, the challenging leadership role creates more of a "competitive atmosphere" and is more performance-oriented. However, I have found that managers who find it difficult to provide demands and goals can find that employees lack this direction. Therefore, in the long run, it is the manager who provides goals and demands that is the popular manager.

The role paradox "delegating–involving"

The delegating–involving role paradox is also found in the results–relationships paradox.

Delegating behavior

Managers who are good at delegating are most often good at being productive, motivated, and dedicated to their tasks. Delegating managers can create an industrious atmosphere in their department, where employees are productive and positively competitive.

Delegating behavior means that each team member takes ownership of his or her tasks and works loyally and productively in order to achieve the goal. A manager needs competences that help to create a "positively competitive" atmosphere within the department. This can be achieved through the following elements:

> The manager goes first in order to set a good example. The manager must be able to show the way through his or her own work ethic as well as commitment and focus on the task. The manager is good at setting and

achieving goals. This means that the manager is good at staying on track, even if there are many other demands and "temptations" to move on to other activities.
> The manager creates meaning within the tasks in collaboration with his or her employees. This is done through explanation using a coaching style. The manager decides *what* needs to happen and the employees decide *how* that will be achieved.
> The manager feels competent and thrives when working with the "irritating" employee who is smarter than the manager. The manager works toward understanding and using the strengths of each employee.

REFLECTION

1. How do you function as a role model for what you want to see in your organization?
2. How can you best communicate why the organization exists and where you need to go (communicate the vision)?
3. What degree of clarity, presence, and dialogue regarding tasks is practiced in your organization/department?
4. To what degree do you communicate with your employees regarding your expectations of results when you give them a project or task?

Confidence is good, and it is especially important in knowledge-intense companies that require employees to have a high degree of autonomy in their work. Most employees like to organize their own work to determine how they will work with and solve problems. The delegating leadership behavior also requires that a manager should actually treat their employees like stars. A manager should simply assume that the employees can do the task, know how to do the task, and will complete the task. However, this required a high level of clarity regarding tasks role and expectations.

This leadership behavior is similar to an element of the situation-based leadership model (Hersey & Blanchard, 1996) called delegation. Delegation arises in a situation where the employees are mature (able to master the task's solution) and are highly motivated to work. In these situations, a manager should try not to get in the way. In this theoretical framework, it is just as much the organizational need that determines to what extent the delegating leadership behavior succeeds.

Involving behavior is located opposite delegating behavior.

Involving behavior

Involvement is created within the team. The manager has the role of a facilitator, and needs to create the opportunity and desire for a shared effort, as well as building collaboration and teamwork. This means that he or she must be good at handling internal conflict and disagreement. In the involving role, the manager must be process-oriented (be able to consciously work to create agreement), have team spirit, and be able to create synergy within the group. This will allow the employees to solve problems and complete tasks by relying on one another.

If the employees are to remain involved, the manager must not be afraid of conflicts, and should believe that honesty is the best way to create connection among the employees.

The following elements make up the focus area for a manager who wants to ensure a high degree of involvement:

> Team-building – bring the various roles to the forefront and create visibility regarding each team member's skills
> Conflict management – work with problems where there is disagreement, competition, and difficulty working together
> Openness – go out on a limb and make sure that the team can discuss everything. This creates the trust that is needed
> Involvement – insist that the team members use their influence; make sure that all opinions and thoughts are shared, especially from those employees who usually don't say much.

The involving leadership behavior makes sure that the employees are a part of the decision-making process, and that democracy is a part of the workplace.

REFLECTION

1. How well does your team function together?
2. How do you work to develop your team and ensure that they coordinate tasks and know where they can get support from one another?
3. How do you work with conflict in the team? Do you intervene early?
4. To what degree do you involve your employees? What types of decisions are they a part of?
5. How well do your employees know what you or the senior management are considering and developing regarding the company?

An involving leadership style contributes to the creation of a high degree of task ownership. Employees are able to commit to the vision and goals and create a shared foundation by being involved in diverse problems and decisions. This allows them to achieve their potential. They are also able to share their ideas, strengths, and resources, which creates a shared sense of well-being and a foundation for working toward the organization's goals.

In this chapter I have used CVF as one option for a guideline for understanding paradoxical thinking. CVF often helps me when I am working as a consultant in order to develop leadership. This is mostly because it is also useful to the managers I work with, and allows us to have a clear structure for the discussions about leadership action. The model contains the different types of leadership behavior that correspond with the organizational paradoxes that were described in Chapters 4 and 5. The model for role paradoxes reflects organizational paradoxes. The eight types of leadership behavior are nothing new. Similar versions with small variations and different terminology can be found in many leadership books. They can be considered common knowledge in the field. However, the reason I have chosen to emphasize them here is the challenge of implementing them. The challenge is to make contradictory demands easier to deal with, to reflect on your own leadership position, to continually question which leadership position is most useful to the organization, and to consider how these leadership roles can *simultaneously* be implemented in the concrete leadership behavior of an organization.

The point of paradoxical thinking is that these leadership elements are simultaneous demands on a manager, not elements that are connected to different managers at different times. However, this is unfeasible in the current leadership practice, because managers constantly turn their backs on an important organizational focus area in order to focus on something else. If managers are able to pay attention to what they turn their backs on or let lie, they can create a conscious and reflective practice rather than a practice of inadequacy. Here is an example:

> A manager in a marketing company was brainstorming regarding her development as a manager. She was a well-liked manager who felt that it was time to start setting demands. I asked why, and she said that the company needed to move in a shared direction. Everyone had been involved in the decision-making process to the degree that the employees had almost become enterprises in themselves. The manager thought that this had affected the shared business profile so much that there was a need for some "collection," as she called it. By collection, she meant a shared goal and direction, which each employee would be required to live up to. Throughout our brainstorming sessions, she used the CVF model to change focus toward delegating and challenging her employees. The organization needed a more result-oriented focus. The manager told her employees about the CVF model and shared her decisions regarding the leadership shift with them. Everyone agreed that it was the right decision. They had also been frustrated over the fact that they did not all have the same understanding of the organization's goal and focus areas.
>
> Later in our brainstorming session, we began to work with how the manager could involve her employees and support collaborative problem-solving, even when they didn't agree about how they should live up to the shared and individual goals. The manager realized that if she wanted to set demands for her employees, she needed to involve and support them in the problem-solving process. The CVF model was primarily used to place focus on what

was needed so that she could strengthen the company's competitive ability in the market. The model created awareness about concepts, and the challenge moved from being a question about leadership tools (I am a manager who is best at supporting employees) to a question of which leadership behavior should be increased and how she should do that. In addition, she could now justify her leadership efforts to both employees and management.

With reference to the discussion about the paradigm bridge in management from Chapter 2, paradoxical thinking means moving away from treating leadership as a personal attribute or personality trait where some managers have a better "match" than others. There is a broad assumption that some managers "just have it" while other managers "just aren't the leadership type." I do not regard leadership in this way. In contrast, I believe that good leadership is situation-dependent, that it depends on the demands of the surroundings and the needs of the organization as well as the changes that are under way at any given moment. This can appear as a "lucky match" between the manager "who just has it" and the organization that is successful. Many managers, both individually and in groups, can fail if their leadership practice is not reflective and intentional. Meaning-making activities as well as a shared leadership language and a shared understanding of leadership as a professional discipline are absolutely necessary in order to fulfill organizational change and create what I will call "useful leadership positions."

Summary

Leadership is a balancing act, but without a leadership concept that can include contradictory demands, leadership initiatives develop toward a private practice approach with the hope that each individual manager will coincidentally get recognition as one of those that "have it."

The CVF model contains elements from the modern and postmodern paradigms. The relationship and change fields correspond to a postmodern approach where new elements are created through dialogue and collaborative processes. The result and stability fields correspond to a modern way of thinking, where leadership behavior is based on guidelines, direction, goal-management and best practice.

REFLECTION: ROLE PARADOXES

1. What are the preferred leadership positions in your management team?
2. How does that contribute to the organization's results?
3. What is the relevant challenge for the organization at the moment?
4. Which leadership positions should you "turn up" in order to match the organization's challenge?
5. How do you discuss this in your management team?

We have now connected concrete leadership positions to the organization's numerous contradictory demands regarding leadership initiatives. In the next chapter, I will provide an example of how a management group used the CVF model as a starting point for adjusting their shared leadership efforts and distributed roles in a way that made the most sense in regard to the needs of the organization.

7
ROLE PARADOXES IN PRACTICE
Examples of leadership development

The narratives in this chapter are examples from my consulting practice, which will illustrate how paradoxical thinking can function as a guide to supporting organizational change through concrete leadership action within the management group. The role paradoxes can be used to guide the dialogue about which leadership action is needed in the management group. In some situations they can be used to work with how the various roles should be distributed in relation to the leadership task (see the case on the "Bird-nest school" (Fuglebakkeskolen) in the next section), and in other situations they are useful for finding out how the collected leadership action should be prioritized in relation to the organization's strategic areas. We will start by looking at an example of how tasks can be understood and distributed within a management team that wants the members to complement each other.

Role paradoxes: toward clarity regarding tasks and roles within the management team

This narrative is about a management team that worked together for a period after a merger, but was unable to become a cohesive unit. We worked with CVF in order to create clarity regarding roles, tasks, and their expectations toward each other. They also began to utilize their individual strengths after they experienced that they had a leadership framework with which to discuss the difficult parts of their teamwork.

>   The Bird-nest School's management team (names are changed) approached us because they wanted to have a coaching session in order to discover shared direction and strengthen themselves as a team.
>   The administration had submitted requirements that the school should be led by a team that consisted of at least one principal, a vice principal, and an

SFO (after-school program) manager. Furthermore, the municipality wanted the management teams to be distributed as much as possible according to grade level – preschool (kindergarten–3rd grade), primary school (3rd–6th grade), and secondary school (7th–9th grade). There was one big school, so the principal, Karsten, did not have the opportunity to participate in teaching because of the demands of the management tasks. The vice principal, Lisbeth, was responsible for the pedagogical and academic elements of the school. The SFO manager, Hanne, had said that she would like to manage the new schooling system for preschool where teachers and other pedagogues would be together with the children the entire day, as opposed to a division between school and SFO.

The school needed to do some visionary work. They needed to figure out how the school should be organized at the preschool level. All three were frustrated (just like the personnel) that the development process had halted and they felt insecure and paralyzed and couldn't move forward. The foundation of the problem was that all three of the managers couldn't understand why the others didn't step up and do something about the problem.

We worked with multiple problems, two of which were especially prominent: the principal, Karsten, and the vice principal, Lisbeth, experienced a lot of ambiguity and friction between the two of them, mostly because Lisbeth was under stress and often out sick. The principal thought that this was a result of Lisbeth working with the wrong tasks. The vice principal had acted as a principal for a while, and during that time she had become aware of the administrative tasks involved with such a role. Karsten believed that Lisbeth was using her time on the wrong tasks. At the same time, Lisbeth had become unpopular and invisible among the personnel, who complained about her performance and were unhappy that she didn't maintain a pedagogical approach or create clarity regarding what she wanted to achieve regarding the school's visions and pedagogy.

The other problem was that the SFO manager, Hanne, "moped about," as the principal characterized it. She asked for an individual conversation with us, and wanted to discuss the problem regarding her own role at the school. She thought that there was a strange atmosphere in the management team and couldn't quite figure out where her two management colleagues were coming from. She felt that they didn't quite include her.

The three managers agreed to complete a MPI profile (Management of Paradox Indicator). MPI is a tool for measuring leadership that I developed together with a colleague, and I use it to find out which leadership behavior the managers demonstrate most in relation to a given organizational situation or strategy. The measurements are based on the CVF model from Chapter 6, and measure the manager's role in relation to the current task.

The profile is made up of 96 questions, and when the manager has completed them, a profile appears which can be analyzed in relation to the CVF wheel (see Figures 7.1–7.3). This allows us and the managers to see

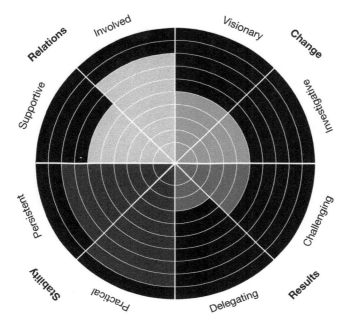

FIGURE 7.1 Current role focus of a leadership team: Karsten

where the preferred leadership action is in the situation. When discussing leadership paradoxes, it is possible for a manager to demonstrate a high level of behavior within stability as well as change, or in both results and people. However, it is also possible to have a low level of behavior in all four parameters.

We used the test to create a discussion within the management team about how roles can be used in relation to the organizational needs in a given situation. At the Bird-nest School, we used the test in order to start a discussion about the level of role distribution regarding what the school might need. The results are shown in Figures 7.1–7.3.

Several parts of the test showed interesting results: In relation to the first problem (the working relationship between Karsten and Lisbeth), the test showed that all three managers were strong in the stability field. The principal and vice principal combined this with a large teamwork focus. Karsten was surprised that Lisbeth's change field wasn't stronger, because his experience was that Lisbeth was hired to develop the academic and pedagogical elements of the school, and he wished that she would do more of that and not spend so much time on his tasks, that he was much better at anyway. Lisbeth was also surprised. She said that she realized that she was working with the wrong things. She had not wanted to leave her principal with the "boring tasks," as she called them. That was why she

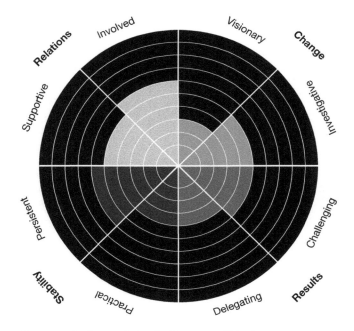

FIGURE 7.2 Current role focus of a leadership team: Lisbeth

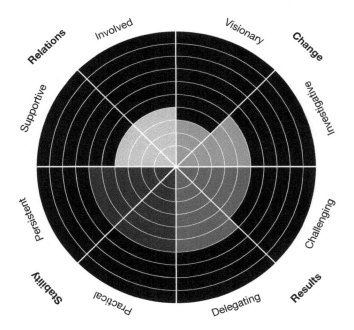

FIGURE 7.3 Current role focus of a leadership team: Hanne

had used more time on administration management than she thought she had time and skills for.

During the dialogue, the two were able to reconcile their expectations, made a plan that they should try to strengthen Lisbeth's change field, and created an action plan (according to the description of the behavior that was related to the change field). This was an eye-opener for Lisbeth, and Karsten also felt that he was finally able to discuss what he expected and what the staff expected.

Afterwards, Lisbeth said that she felt "reinstated" in her role, in that it had always been defined, but not completed. Already while in the brainstorming sessions, Lisbeth began to work with how she could involve a project group of teachers and other pedagogues in order to investigate which academic areas the preschool should work with in the future, and what that would mean for the teachers and pedagogues.

In relation to the other problem (the SFO manager, Hanne's, problem with her leadership role), Hanne's insecurity was reflected in her profile. She had an understanding of herself as a person who was very good at communicating with the staff and helping them work together and be organized in order to create a thriving and efficient work environment. However, her leadership behavior was decidedly unspecific. We later discussed that Hanne felt that she wasn't being used to her potential and she felt excluded from the management due to her pedagogical background. She couldn't figure out what the other two managers' expectations were of her.

It then came out that from the start, Karsten and Lisbeth had thought that Hanne shouldn't be the after-school program manager, because the teachers had said that they weren't ready to have a pedagogue as a manager. This discussion clarified things for Hanne. Among other things, she realized that the other two managers wanted to have a discussion with her regarding where she saw herself in the team, and if her management of the after-school program should be shared with the teachers. Hanne needed some time to relate to their responses, and felt that it was best to discuss her role in a separate meeting.

It was agreed that Karsten should develop a suggestion of how he saw Hanne's role in the SFO and the school as a whole. Karsten also identified a need for Hanne to work on the development of the new preschool system in collaboration with someone from the teachers' team.

When I talked with Hanne later on, she had gotten a clearer profile. The clarity that was provided in relation to the expectations of her as a manager (including what wasn't expected) meant that she was able to work with developing visions together with her coworkers, involving coworkers, and starting activities where visions and new approaches could be explored. This allowed the after-school program to have a new role in the preschool model that was on the horizon. Hanne became more visible through these visionary and collaborative dimensions, which was exactly what the school needed.

This case shows how two management levels in a workplace can work together using paradoxes as a starting point. The principal and vice principal were able to discuss their leadership action – not in the form of personalities and static leadership action, but in the form of the positions they expected or expected one another to embody. The MPI was used as a concrete tool to coordinate the leadership actions so that the school's needs were met in the best possible way. Both managers needed to adjust their leadership action in accordance with the school's need for them to contribute in a different way.

There are, of course, many other ways to approach such a dialogue within a management team. The dialogue that was seen at the "Bird-nest" School had its starting point in an organizational reality that required both the postmodern and modern leadership styles. As I discussed in Chapter 2, it is important that an organization's management works simultaneously with both the modern and postmodern values. The ability to be able to move into other leadership positions when necessary is only an option when there is a shared set of concepts to start from. At the "Bird-nest" School, the issue was how the managers could best distribute their areas of responsibility as well as how they could define the expectations on the SFO manager.

The above narrative illustrates how role paradoxes gave rise to a distribution of the workload as well as clarity regarding role distribution within a management team. A dialogue about role paradoxes becomes even more relevant in situations where managers disagree and stick with their own position (which represents their contradictory values). When this happens, the managers lose focus of the fact that they are all in a situation where the paradox needs to be navigated, and where "either-or" thinking is inadequate.

Role paradoxes: toward mutual understanding within the management team

The following narrative is an example of how conflicts can be understood in relation to the organization's competing values:

> The IT company, Systemize, had a management team consisting of four people. One of these managers had been employed for a year, while one of the other managers had been there for 15 years. Conflicts had started between them, and I worked with them in order to find a way for them to respect each other better and achieve synergy that would benefit the entire company. The senior director wanted them to be able to find a way to agree and utilize each other's strengths in order to benefit the company.
>
> Ulla, who had been there for 15 years, wanted to explain that she felt upset, degraded, and provoked by the fact that Peter, who had been there for under a year, came in and, almost from the first day, acted with utmost confidence and thundered around implementing a new approach. She felt that

he did this without "taking the temperature of the organization" and seeing where the employees were. She felt he did not coordinate with, nor involve her, in the goals and action plans for the employees, which were, in fact, her employees. She felt "run over," and had a feeling that she was "backward" and conservative, while she herself thought that she had always been good at creating changes, but doing so by keeping in mind that everyone needed to be included, and that the projects were planned and prioritized in relation to the allowances of the company.

Peter was surprised by this. He had often noticed that Ulla seemed irritated, but he hadn't thought about what might be wrong. He put it down to "adversity," that she maybe wasn't able to handle things, and that she might be jealous because he achieved so many results that the director liked.

When I interviewed Ulla and Peter individually, I asked them which values were important to them in order to succeed in their task, which was to increase profits on the projects they delivered to customers. Here is a list of their answers:

Ulla said:

1. That we ensure order, quality, and stable services
2. That the customers can count on us
3. That the employees can handle it
4. That new projects are prioritized in relation to what we are already doing
5. That we let some things go and agree about which things we choose to deal with
6. That it is better to work with fewer elements so that people are on the same page, and we are sure that we're doing it right, rather than just starting a lot of projects and losing customers

Peter said:

- That we succeed in achieving our goals
- That we make progress on our agreements
- That the employees understand what they need to achieve
- That we start tasks and follow up to ensure that the employees have a good start
- That we reward action
- That we do something! We need to try something new, because right now we are only surviving by pressurizing the organization!

After this conversation, we talked about organizational paradoxes, and about how both truths could exist side by side. Ulla and Peter each represented an end of something they could see was a result of contradictory pressures from the organization.

We discussed that both contradictory ends of the paradox should be implemented in order for development and quality to coexist (change–stability paradox). This developed into a conversation about how the managers could focus on the results field. At the same time, achieving those results required the managers to focus on creating a well-functioning and involved team who supported each other and felt involved in the creation of goals (relationships–results paradox).

Ulla had become tired of always being the one "putting on the brakes" in order to make sure that internal elements functioned (stability and relationships), and that all parties agreed to meet and decide how they could balance the contradictory pressures they were feeling. How should the new approaches be prioritized? Which approach should be started out of all the approaches that were suggested during management meetings? How could Ulla and Peter collaborate to ensure stability and organization when development was also required? How should they lead in order to ensure that the employees understood the goals and felt supported in achieving those goals?

In other words, the parties chose to help one another make a coordinated effort to implement leadership positions between both relationships and results.

Summary

In both cases, the leadership role paradoxes became clear to the management team. The use of the CVF model created a basis for discussing how the managers could work together to implement both sets of values. In the second case, Ulla and Peter were both softened toward the "opposition" and could see that they each sat and guarded their values, when, in fact, both sets of values were needed if the organization was to succeed. As a consultant, I would call this an "externalization" of the problem. It was no longer about personal conflict and personal values, but instead that Peter and Ulla each related to their own end of the values spectrum in relation to the implementation of the organization's strategy.

REFLECTION: REFLECTIVE LEADERSHIP ROLES

1. How can we best describe the task we need to complete in the near future?
2. Which leadership focus do we have right now? What kind of result does this focus provide?
3. Which leadership adjustments should the management team make in order to succeed with our strategy?
4. Which leadership position do I need to strengthen in order to support the strategy as much as possible?
5. To what degree should we all place focus there? To what degree should I attempt to focus on the "opposite" end of the paradox?
6. What does that mean for my leadership behavior?

The CVF model can best be used to create a framework for the management team to work with in order to collectively define the management task. It also provides an opportunity to discuss how the team can lead intentionally in accordance with the goals required for the organization to succeed in the current situation.

Both narratives (the "Bird-nest" School and Systemize) show organizational change, which resulted in the managers relating to management by asking, "What does the organization need to achieve in the near future? What focus do we have now? What does it mean that we should increase leadership? What does it mean that each of us in the management team should have more focus on being a leader?"

In this chapter, I have described the "Bird-nest" School as an example of how managers can use paradoxical leadership to supplement each other in the various roles in a workplace. I then described Systemize as an example of how a management team had begun to polarize leadership roles and represent the various leadership values individually rather than collectively. We saw that a dialogue about the change processes of the organization allowed the managers to see how they could work together to balance the demands between results and relationships. Paradoxical thinking can be used in both situations. However, I have most often used paradoxical thinking in the field between strategic deliberation and the management team's collective leadership effort, as we saw in the second example.

Although Quinn and Cameron claim that CVF encapsulates all the important leadership positions in an organization, I believe that the model is more humble. I understand and utilize it as a model that offers some concepts with which to think flexibly about variable leadership roles. This thinking demands that managers continually read the organization's needs, so that they can implement the appropriate leadership positions to meet these needs. However, the model is far from an exhaustive list of the leadership paradoxes that can be experienced in the organization and in management.

In the next chapter, I will present the third form of paradoxes: the paradoxes of belonging. The paradoxes of belonging are examples of the many types of paradoxes that cannot be described by a single model, but instead describe much more complicated positions.

8
PARADOX OF BELONGING
The emotional aspect

As we saw in the previous chapter, both organizational paradoxes and role paradoxes allow management to reflect on and navigate the paradoxes they find, either as aspects of organizational change or as contradictory demands of their position as a leader in accordance with the ambitions of the organization.

While organizational and role paradoxes indicate basic conditions and problems "within the job," the paradox of belonging addresses the emotional dimension of leadership. Emotions are important in determining how we conduct ourselves in organizations. In this chapter, we will investigate which emotional paradoxes can affect your leadership behavior. We will explore the importance of working to understand yourself as well as the ambivalent feelings that can arise as a result of having to make difficult decisions, think about the whole rather than your own department, work with team development, etc. Your sense of belonging often presents itself in relation to ambivalence regarding how you should relate to others. Let me give you an example:

When negotiating complex processes of change, it is common to distinguish between employees who support the change and those who either oppose the change or are not yet ready to move forward. However, this distinction often creates a rift between employees, even though most employees will, in fact, feel a mixture of support and skepticism. Managers who have been through organizational change will recognize that there is a tendency for some employees to represent the possibilities of change and loyally work to implement these possibilities, while others represent the existing, the "old," and the stable.

I would claim that these different ways of relating to change are often interpreted conservatively by senior management or the organization's theorists that discuss opposition to change. Most managers and employees are able to see the nuances in change. However, if you are in an organization that expects simple, one-dimensional, rational thinking, you will typically embody the positions that support one side of the change–stability paradox. This atmosphere is infectious. It results in some members of the organization representing the ignorance, insecurity, and focus on maintaining known values from the old organization, while others represent the longing for new ideas, optimizing organization, and perhaps even a change to improve the organization and their own positions. At its most fundamental level, change creates ambivalence and tension among the organization's members: both management and employees. However, when we think in terms of "either-or," people distribute themselves along those lines: some support and some oppose.

Lego's paradoxes of belonging

In the Lego project, I named these emotional paradoxes "paradoxes of belonging" because they often involved the ways managers connected emotionally to one another, the organization, management, and their tasks during organizational change. These paradoxes arose during organizational change and include: trust versus control, popularity versus unpopularity, insecurity in their job versus new challenging opportunities, personal interests versus communal interests, and optimism versus focus on problems. These are all types of ambivalence and emotional tension that can be understood as paradoxes in the way people feel that they belong within the organization.

Manager groups can monitor paradoxes of belonging in relation to their own management team, as well as in relation to the contradictory demands of ensuring the success of a department, while still maintaining the interests of the whole. Table 8.1 shows some of the paradoxes of belonging experienced by the Lego managers.

The Lego managers and I found that it was useful for them to be able to share their emotional ambivalence, and therefore be able to recognize it, even if they couldn't immediately see a solution. We discovered that the only useful way for the managers to relate to the paradoxes of belonging was to confront them in order to see the interests and emotions that were involved in the process of change. Through this confrontation, they were able to own the paradoxes as part of their experience.

This resulted in the managers being able to consciously avoid communication that was too clear or too ambiguous in relation to the employees, each other, and themselves. For example, the Lego managers identified the importance of acknowledging the fear of losing control because they were ultimately responsible for the department. However, they also recognized that they needed to allow people to make independent decisions in order for the department to succeed. They were able to discuss the fact that they needed to have some form of control, but that it should be delivered without causing people to feel dominated.

If the managers had not been able to share their ambivalence regarding trust verses control with their employees, they might have said, "You should just function as an autonomous team. Make decisions yourselves, and I, of course, have full confidence that you will make the best decisions due to your professionalism and good sense."

TABLE 8.1 Paradoxes of belonging

The problem →	The dilemma →	The paradox →	→ Toward workable certainty
How do we become a management group that cooperates well?	Should I do what the others are doing **or** should I do things my own way?	Do things as a team **and** do things in your own way	How can we create acceptance of each other (to create common ground) – **and** create acceptance of the fact that we are different?
How can we achieve enough trust for one another in this team?	Should I say what I think **or** should I hold back and make sure I'm accepted?	Individuality **and** team formation	I must try to share some of my own problems with the team and see if we can work on a solution as a group. But will they respect me if I reveal my problem?
Should I discuss additional changes now, even if I don't think that it's right for my team? They can't handle any more changes!	Should I hold back and be loyal to my team **or** should I introduce the new approach and challenge them more?	Be a representative for senior management **and** be loyal to the employees	I will discuss how we can continue to be good at our jobs and still take on yet another task for change.

It can be beneficial to share the trust side of the paradox, but if you are still afraid of losing control, you will demonstrate controlling behavior regardless, even though you said something else. I have often seen managers who talk about autonomous teams and yet clearly still want to figure out how they can be in control so that the organization can succeed.

This can cause problems between the manager and the employees. Because the manager can't avoid communicating his or her intentions to the employees (also through actions), he or she will end up demonstrating a lack of trust in the employees. For example, if the manager asks for documentation reports and meetings with feedback, the employees will feel attacked, and feel that the responsibility they have been given isn't actually genuine.

If this happens, the employees will become passive and stop taking initiative, which will therefore confirm the manager's belief that close monitoring and repeated directions to the employees is necessary for them to act "independently." The trust–control paradox is clearly apparent here.

The paradox of belonging can create a pattern of communication that is called a self-strengthening loop. As long as the manager continues to insist that employees show initiative and independence, but simultaneously demonstrates control and monitoring, the employees will continue to adjust and attempt to conform to the framework provided by the manager. This will demonstrate to the manager that the employees are unable to act independently and he or she will therefore feel that there is an increased need for control. This pattern of interaction strengthens itself. The manager creates contradictory actions because ambivalence is split between trust and control and, without discussion of the situation, what is expressed as trust ends up feeling like control.

Sometimes, this type of contradictory message cannot be discussed within the group. Instead, a specific method of relating to one another is shared: "It's so nice that our group is so open. We can improve the way in which we share knowledge, but the intention is there." This can be the managers' attempt to "conjure" trust. In addition, this can be their attempt to "dull" the paradox between trust and control because it is hard to deal with the fact that both feelings should be present at the same time. There is focus on trust, but it is not acceptable to address the need to be careful and maintain control.

In those situations where it is not possible to discuss reservations, or in situations where it isn't a good idea to share knowledge, managers can use other methods to create understanding. However, the paradox is still there: If I go along with pretending that I am becoming more open, then I'm not open about how I feel. But if I say that I need to maintain control of the knowledge I have, then I'm still not being open. When a manager says, "I think that we are open (even though you all say something else)," he or she is expressing a self-inhibiting contradiction. It's not really feasible to discuss such a statement. This paradoxical type of communication is called a double bind.

Here is another example from Lego: The managers were forced to admit that they could be afraid of not achieving good results in their own departments when they have to give staff to the others. However, being able to discuss these things in the management team allowed them to avoid taking their fears out on one another. They were able to work with acknowledging and standing firm in their ambivalence in lending personnel to other departments. One way this was done was through each manager personally addressing the loss he or she felt when lending out a large number of employees. Discussing the issue could help the other managers to find a balance between the individual need to have a department succeed, and the need to succeed in helping each other as a whole. The emotional aspects were difficult, but not impossible, to share and use to create meaning.

The paradoxes of belonging encompass the emotional aspects of being in groups, departments, and organizations. In their book, *Paradoxes of Group Life*, Smith & Berg (1987) write that paradoxes exist as emotions, experiences, and the values of individuals and groups, and that they exist in all groups. By this they mean that individuals experience groups and communities as entities filled with contradictions and contradictory emotions, thoughts, and actions.

Although managers attempt to be completely unambiguous and direct, ambivalence will always show itself through words and actions. Feelings strengthen our actions, whether we want them to or not. If we try to eliminate them, they only become stronger: "A powerful, albeit unconscious threat to the group is that only one side of the group members' reactions to being in the group will be allowed expression" (Smith & Berg, 1987, p. 25).

Smith & Berg argue that the more ambivalence is denied, the greater ambiguity becomes. If a manager doesn't want to share his or her knowledge with the team, because knowledge is power, the team management will often attempt to point out that the team has rules for openness and sharing. Rules can be made to ensure that knowledge is shared. This will force team members to share, but only enough to show that they know something, not enough to be able to use that knowledge. People will share more when there is more pressure to share knowledge, but there will also be an increase in the amount of elements that are held back and not shared.

There is only one alternative to these self-strengthening patterns: to talk about what isn't trusted and what people don't want to share. It is important that a group can also talk about what is in the way and what is at risk.

Some management teams feel that it is very difficult to discuss these things. It is true that this is difficult, but stopping the habit of splitting the paradoxes and stating "that knowledge should be shared" or that "we need to show trust" often contributes significantly to clarity within the organization. If members of an organization can talk about these problems, they can also work to balance their emotions. If, on the other hand, these problems are not discussed, the organization will end up talking about clarity, but creating ambiguity between the contradictions that lie between what is said and what is done.

The tool: dialogue about ambivalence

Investigating what various members of an organization are focusing on during a process of change reveals that each member often fights for different values. At first glance, these different values can appear to be contradictory, but each contains elements of truth. If you want to ensure that your organization's change is as smooth as possible, you should have an overview of how you support or avoid this split, or in other words, how much you support an "either-or" way of thinking. You must then challenge yourself to achieve a paradoxical perspective, so that you can create meaning from the contradictory values and demonstrate how others can see paradoxes as well as relate to the nuances of how the old can include the new, and vice versa. Here is an example:

> A consulting firm in a challenging competitive market informed its employees that the company was going to merge with another company, which was located in two other areas of the country. The director, administration, and

company headquarters would be located in the largest city. A tour for all the employees of the "new company" was arranged so that they could get to know one another. During the tour, the employees were informed that the company would be creating a new work culture that would integrate the strengths and cultural characteristics of the old company.

After a few months, a number of employees in the other two locations took sick leave or quit the company. This led to management questioning what had happened to cause this. In connection with a session about how to create a good merger, I was able to investigate what was going on for those employees who were on sick leave or who had chosen to quit the company.

I realized that there was a situation where there was double communication regarding the merger. The employees of the "previous" offices were frustrated that management continually informed them that this was an equal merger, that nothing would change (other than there would be a synergy effect from merging), that employees would be able to take advantage of the larger scale of the company, etc. Yet they experienced that the style of management had changed, employee relationships were adjusted by headquarters, that people from the merged department were the ones being fired, etc. As one employee said in an interview, "It's as if they just called it a merger because they wanted us to like it, but in reality it is a take-over. We just can't talk about it like that, because they deny it, and then you just feel more insecure and give them the impression that you are against what's going on. But we are actually starting to be against it, because we don't have any real opportunities to talk about the disparities that are happening. It could be okay to have disparities, but they keep acting like it is an equal merger and keep claiming that it is, even though it doesn't feel that way at all to us. But I shouldn't have said anything, because next time it will be me that is fired, or labeled 'non-compliant'…"

After interviewing several employees from "the other" departments, I had a feedback session with management, where we worked with helping the managers to confront their own ambiguous statements and their unwillingness to involve the "smaller" companies in the process of creating a shared culture. We discussed the big-brother/little-brother dynamic (which is often connected to mergers/take-overs), and management began to examine their unwillingness and realized that they had difficulty demonstrating trust in the other departments. They realized that this was because they were afraid that the other departments would become too disconnected and autonomous if they were given more control and the ability to work independently. At the same time, management was dependent on employees and department managers collaborating with the process, since the central management wasn't able to control and oversee as much at the other locations.

The management group's paradox of trust and control was verbalized, and a dialogue process was begun in order to inform the department managers about which parts of the process should be left up to the individual departments, and which parts would be determined by headquarters. One conclusion was that these companies had been successfully autonomous for many years, so management should investigate how much trust they could show the individual departments, and therefore arrange ways to have a continuous oversight of what was happening in each department. This would allow the departments to learn more about each other and inspire each other.

The trust–control paradox was identified through confrontations and self-reflections among the management group. It became clear to the management group that they needed to reflect on the elements of communication, which were supposed to be clear statements, but contained some contradictions, which therefore led to ambivalence among middle management and the employees.

In situations such as these, it is important that management has the courage to examine the ambivalence and ambiguities they are expressing, even when this may not be "opportune" for the company's clarity and direction. In order to be able to manage these types of situations, managers must have the courage to confront the emotional tensions that result from paradoxes of belonging. In the example above, it was important that management was confident (to be able to stand by the merger and see it through), and impressionable (to be able to find and manage the problems that occur throughout the process). Management's primary task is to help employees and middle management continually create meaning from the contradictory demands and contradictory and ambiguous communication that makes up an organization. Ambiguous communication, contradictions, and paradoxes cannot be avoided, even in a process that is thoroughly planned and checked.

In other words, the management group needs to be able to confront themselves and reflect on the various unplanned problems that arise during the change process that determine whether or not everyone is on board with the process.

Workable certainty implies that management need to start with themselves. This is because communication within the organization reflects tension within management. If the managers reflect on what is happening within the group, they will be ready to define paradoxes and lead with complexity as a companion, rather than an obstacle. Complexity and paradoxes become much easier to manage once they can be discussed.

My claim is that all processes of change are dependent on managers who:

1. Continually analyze and understand their own ambivalence, ambiguities, and confusions.
2. Use these paradoxical emotions in order to define the existing paradoxes, and take them into account when determining leadership action.
3. Discuss this with the employees.

Many management groups have become rational and formal, without being in contact with the fundamental emotional complexity that is a part of organizational change. However, accepting insecurity and confronting the emotional aspects of the tasks that create this insecurity will allow management to work within the paradox, and therefore provide more clarity.

The purpose of confronting a management group's contradictory feelings and experiences is to be able to integrate the emotional with the rational. An analysis of defensive reactions and ambiguous experiences allows management to be able to maintain a paradoxical perspective and therefore manage the contradictions and ambiguities as an integrated part of the organization's change. We can find a well-known example of the paradox of belonging in leadership theory. This example is the Stockdale paradox, which is a bit blunt, but shows how the realism–optimism paradox can be managed by avoiding unilateral optimism.

The Stockdale paradox

Managers who want to work with dramatic change of opinions and behavior can often feel that "this is too much." Employees are split and managers can lose faith in the hope of things ever improving. Many larger processes of change enter periods where the process becomes unmanageable, managers feel powerless, and there is a demand for participation *and* clear statements as well as autonomy *and* strong leadership, etc.

The Stockdale paradox illustrates this situation. The paradox is named after Vice Admiral James Bond Stockdale, who was the highest ranked officer to be captured during the Vietnam War. Stockdale and his troops were held prisoner and tortured for eight years in the infamous prison, the "Hanoi Hilton" (as it was sarcastically known). Stockdale said that he never lost faith that he would escape alive and that the experience would prove to be the most important aspect of his life. On the other hand, Stockdale never avoided acknowledging the brutal reality and the cold hard facts during his captivity.

Stockdale felt that it was this ability to confront both aspects of the situation at the same time that helped him survive. He was able to believe that he would survive while constantly being confronted with the seriousness of the situation. When an interviewer asked him, "Who was it that didn't make it out?" Stockdale answered:

> This is a very important lesson. You must never confuse *faith* that you will prevail in the end – which you can never afford to lose – with the *discipline* to confront the most brutal facts of your current reality, whatever they might be.
> *Collins (2001, p. 85)*

In other words, just hoping you will survive is not enough; you have to actually do the hard stuff in order to get there. So, the Stockdale paradox is the necessity of having both faith and discipline – both the optimism that you will succeed and the realistic determination to do what needs to be done. It's a paradox because optimism – something essential to your success – can be your undoing if applied in excess or without some realism.

The book *Good to Great* (Collins, 2001) builds on an investigation of the factors that help a company move from being good to being great. The book concludes that the Stockdale paradox is an important element in managing difficult changes. Managers must use the Stockdale paradox throughout processes of change: Maintain a steadfast belief that the organization will succeed in the end, and that the process of change will achieve its goals regardless of the opposition, but simultaneously be able to recognize reality and the brutal facts of the situation, and work tirelessly towards managing reality.

The quote below shows that the paradox can also be used in relation to changes in management in Danish companies. The quote is from an interview with Lego's administrative director, Jørgen Vig Knudstorp, from *Børsen*, September 9, 2005 ("Lego must learn the art of the impossible" "Lego skal laere det umuliges kunst").

> We communicate brutally internally, and aren't afraid to say something when we see poor results. We also try to praise people when something goes well, but I think that many employees feel that senior management is sometimes quite negative. To be honest, it's because we want everything out in the open so everyone can see that things aren't okay. We need to look up the mountain instead of standing on top of the mountain and looking down. We really want people to understand that this is a cutthroat business, and that we have to keep working.

The Stockdale paradox demonstrates that employees who only focus on optimism will not support organizational change, because this way of thinking implies hope rather than action. Strong leadership means confronting the uncomfortable facts and starting to change them, regardless of the discouraging elements of reality. For the past several years, leadership literature has focused on how success comes to those who focus on strengths and successful elements of an organization. The employees who accept change without criticism or objection are the ones who succeed and are promoted, because they always agree with the boss and can't see anything but good tactics and opportunities within the company. However, these employees can be compared to the optimists of the Stockdale paradox: If change is built only through optimism among managers and employees, the company risks forgetting to confront some of the inconveniences and more negative sides of change. Challenges must be seen and recognized in order for things to change.

The Stockdale paradox means that managers and management groups will go farthest by believing that things will succeed, while simultaneously confronting themselves and each other with the ambivalence, ambiguities, and two-sided objectives and tasks that arise in all processes of change.

Workable certainty through the paradox of belonging

What can be done to find shared clarity and empowerment? Leadership theories offer many approaches, but paradoxes of belonging and double-sided beliefs must be confronted in order for them to be managed logically. The confrontation with paradoxes and ambivalence is a way to connect rational thinking with the implicit irrational elements of a situation. Most paradox theorists view this as the first step in the direction of being able to manage and act within this dichotomy.

According to Vince & Broussine (1996), the first step in confrontation is to address your own defense mechanisms. Defense can be seen as different ways to avoid opposition, contradiction, and discomfort. The intent is to decrease discomfort, increase meaning, and avoid an "unsolvable" problem. Defense mechanisms are traditionally considered as psychological and unconscious mechanisms that serve the purpose of creating clarity and calm within the system. The problem is that they only create temporary calm with individuals, and the problems don't disappear. The demands and opposition are still there, but are simply attributed to the lack of clarity from senior management, colleagues, or employees.

Smith & Berg (1987) state that confrontation with contradictory feelings and potential conflicts provides the opportunity to realize that contradictory feelings are still connected. The apparently contradictory feelings that are experienced in an organization under change should be discussed. In the Lego example, the theme was being in a new management team where the managers needed to think collaboratively *and* competitively in order to succeed well enough to survive a future round of lay-offs. They found it liberating to discuss how these elements could exist side by side.

Leadership in paradoxes of belonging

In contrast to role paradoxes, paradoxes of belonging are difficult to talk about. According to Smith and Berg, discussion of paradoxes of belonging can best be initiated by an outside person (consultant, other manager, etc.), who can help with the process because they do not represent any elements of the paradox. Working with paradoxes of belonging means taking ownership of the emotional and casual thoughts that have been hidden, polarized, or simplified. This ownership allows for an investigation of the inherent ambivalence and complexity connected to paradoxes. Lewis & Dehler (2000) claim that such an investigation demands delving into extremes and approaching feelings of insecurity, mistrust, and anxiety. These feelings direct many of our managerial decisions (for example, "Should I share knowledge with the others in my management team or should I use that knowledge to stay ahead?").

The goal of this process is to be able to manage the paradox, to be able to live with it, and to realize how you can compete and collaborate in an organization. This realization will allow you to overcome the double-sided fear that you will fail if you do things on your own, but that you will also fail if you give too much to others.

Paradoxes of belonging have often been called "cross-pressures." However, the concept of paradoxes of belonging moves the focus from the pressures faced by employees, and instead highlights the *emotional* dimensions of the paradoxes that can make it even more difficult to escape them. For example, a central issue for many companies is the cross-pressure between working on behalf of senior management and simultaneously being dependent on the trust and loyalty of the employees. When working with this paradox of belonging, the important element is that the manager feels trapped by having to be disobedient in order to do what is expected.

It can be advantageous for a management group to consult with an external facilitator in order to create clarity when working with the paradoxes of belonging. This could be an external consultant, but it could also be a manager from a completely different place in the organization (such as a manager consultant from the HR department). The most important thing is that it is someone who can question the basic assumptions of understanding and acting within the organization. Here is an example:

> Lego's management group was struggling to create an agenda that could be shared with and be relevant to everyone. This was difficult work, and the members of the meeting began to question the fundamental meaning behind the structure of the team. The senior manager said that he didn't know how he should involve the team members and create synergy in the team when no one contributed to the meetings. As a rule, he was the one who ended up bringing up relevant information and making decisions. He had associations with the previous organization, which was much more hierarchical. In the previous organization, the meetings were more instructive and had less of a dialogue.
>
> I asked the team members what they thought the manager could do to involve them. This question opened up for a shared, albeit slightly sluggish, exploration of what the managers experienced as a desire to be involved, combined with an insecurity about how they should act in the management team. The paradox of belonging was relevant here because the managers longed to be visible while still being afraid of being too visible and risking failure. We were able to identify the tension between these desires and therefore formulated the paradox as, "Someone needs to take the first step before they can find out whether it was worth taking the step." At some point, the senior manager (who was also a member of the team) said, "I think I need to show the others some of my insecurities and then see if there is anyone who follows me. Maybe I should question some of the things that I am not completely clear about." In other words, the senior manager discovered that if he took the first step and demonstrated the desired behavior within the team, it might be possible for others to feel able to disclose their conflicting experiences. This could then allow them to experiment with ways to begin to use the team to create more clarity.
>
> Another example was the manager who insisted that the team should work closely together to complete their tasks, but who simultaneously praised the employee of the month, gave individual rewards, and identified the employees that were doing the best. Again and again he told the employees that they

must work in a collaborative team, and they agreed, but this never happened in practice.

I confronted him with this pattern in a brainstorming session, and we found that he was caught in the paradox of belonging of competition versus collaboration. From this point, we could discuss how he could provide rewards in situations where he felt that employees were motivated by individual as well as collective performance. We made a plan in order to determine how these reward systems could incorporate both motivations.

A final example was the manager who informed his employees that he expected them to be more autonomous, but who still got involved or took over when mistakes were made or something didn't go according to plan. How could the employees take responsibility when they knew that in the end there was only one way to do things, which was how the manager would have done them? This is an example of another paradox of belonging: trust versus control. The manager was caught between showing trust to his employees while still wanting to control them.

Paradoxes of belonging are difficult to discuss, yet they forcefully drive our actions. As we saw in Chapter 3, there are many examples of double binds, or situations where contradictory elements can't be discussed. For example, if employees say that the manager takes over whenever they try to do things by themselves, this can show distrust of the manager. The manager can then feel forced to say that, of course he trusts the employees, but they don't live up to his trust, and therefore he is forced to intervene. It is difficult for many managers to recognize that taking over in these situations does not demonstrate trust. In addition, the manager might be feeling pressure to create results in his or her department, which can lead to a feeling that he or she has to have more control when it appears that "the trust hasn't been met." In this situation, the manager might say, "Yeah, but this shows that I *can't* trust them." At the same time, the employees might say, "You act like we are people you can't trust." This situation exemplifies the paradoxical message of "being autonomous" (meaning that *I* am the one who evaluates when you are being autonomous).

Summary

We have now examined paradoxes of belonging – the emotional paradoxes that managers must relate to as part of the leadership discipline. Part of managing paradoxical situations and ambivalence is confronting the emotional tension and potential conflicts that are experienced in the organization. This occurs when individuals and members of the management team focus only on one side of the paradox of belonging. Management must be self-critical and continually challenge their ways of understanding change. This requires managerial self-reflection and confrontation with contradictions. This can be done through recognizing that there is a degree of discomfort when identifying places where ambiguity, contradiction, and paradoxes are reflected within communication. The question is whether the management team is ready to accept this discomfort or rather remain in the fog of ambiguity. It is not easy to set the more ambivalent themes on the agenda.

Confronting paradoxes of belonging is difficult because of their strong emotional components. In essence, confrontation means that the team needs to discuss the "undiscussable." Here are some examples of questions that can help start this process:

REFLECTION: PARADOXES OF BELONGING

1. Which communication patterns can we see in the organization right now?
2. What do we achieve when we communicate in that way? What is positive? What is negative?
3. What is difficult to do clearly, in regard to senior management/employees/each other? (For example, knowledge-sharing, borrowing employees, assisting with each other's projects, etc.)
4. What are the taboo subjects in the organization?
5. What type of ambivalence do I have in regard to taking the next step?

These questions will be the first step toward managing, and sharing, the complexity of contradictory feelings and the sense of belonging that exists in the organization. The next step is to recognize how this is discussed among the employees and management group. Without this understanding, there is a risk of focusing on who is "right," and the "good" employees who focus on the more positive side of the paradox, versus who is "against" and therefore the "bad" employees. The point is that both positions contain important messages that should be discussed in order to integrate them while working with change.

In the next chapter I will provide some practical narrations that reflect how the paradox of belonging is expressed, and how it can be an impetus so that management and employees can navigate the complexities of the paradox of belonging.

9
THE PARADOXES OF BELONGING IN PRACTICE

Moving toward relationships and a well-functioning management team

The narratives in this chapter revolve around situations that force managers and management groups to confront the ambivalence, double binds, tensions, and contradictory feelings that are found in relation to being a member of an organization undergoing change. I will provide some examples of how paradoxes of belonging are at play, and how they can be worked with in management groups and leadership development. Trust and the ability to collaborate in the management team are essential for managers to be able to have the courage to discuss the emotional aspects, or lack thereof, that affect decisions.

The paradox of belonging: trust–control

Unimotor is the result of the merger of two companies within the same branch. For many years, the company had a director who was very headstrong, who made decisions and didn't communicate about them, but who always expected that the employees did exactly what he had decided. No one felt especially involved, and the employees were seldom asked for advice in regard to strategy or new approaches.

After the merger, Eric became director. Eric had a reputation for being very directive, headstrong, and difficult to get close to, but also for being very good at rectifying companies that were "limping" in the market. I knew Eric from my work with other companies, and I was invited to create a development session with the six members of the senior management group. The goal was to bring them together and make them into a stronger team.

Eric wanted to work with his leadership style. He wanted to involve his senior management team, and he truly believed that he could run the company better in collaboration with the team than he could alone. In fact, he felt dependent on their engagement in the decision-making processes of the company in order for these decisions to live up to the company's strategy. However, Eric's experience was that the senior management team often ended up thinking of their own departments, and therefore they were not reaching their potential or achieving the desired focus on the business perspective of the company as whole. This resulted in "silo-thinking," which caused Eric to feel pressured to be tough, headstrong, and trust only his own decisions.

Eric explained to his senior management team that he needed the other five members of the team, and that he expected the team to work together, and that everyone had a responsibility to influence the direction of the company and the decisions that needed to be made. In the introductory meeting, Eric said, "First and foremost, I expect that you all will participate in the running of this business. You are subsequently managers for your individual departments, but your focus should always be, first and foremost, on the business as a whole."

We established three types of activities during the session: brainstorming sessions with Eric, process facilitation in management group meetings, and individual brainstorming sessions with the individual department managers.

The paradox of belonging quickly became apparent in the sessions. Two problems arose:

1. The senior managers seldom contributed in the management meetings. They didn't say much apart from reporting from their department and then agreeing with Eric's suggested approaches. The agreement was that the managers should bring issues to the meeting that influenced the entire business, but this was not happening, and Eric began to realize that this was a well-known state of his team. How could it be that the managers became more and more docile and/or silent as time went on?
2. The managers did not approach Eric with the diverse problems that affected the company, as they had agreed. Eric had identified the fact that he needed to be updated, and that the managers needed to share their various problems with him so that he could maintain oversight and make the correct decisions.

> During a brainstorming session with a senior manager from the service department, I discovered that Eric held meetings with individual senior managers in between management group meetings, in order to talk about how each individual manager was doing. He kept a close eye on how the individual department performed, and he controlled the revenue and budget of each department. The service manager said that one of the reasons he didn't say so much was that he didn't agree with the plan of transferring tasks to the project-sales department, because they weren't as effective as his own department. He also said that he knew that if he transferred assignments to the project-sales department, he would have to answer to Eric. However, he would rather have the benefit of being able to create his own departmental

budget. He felt that no matter what was agreed, he wouldn't risk his own budgets.

I discovered that his type of problem was widespread among the senior management group. The managers guarded their own positions in the company, and only concentrated on the success of their individual departments.

Eric and his senior management team began to work with this is two ways: The first was through a brainstorming session with Eric. In this session, I confronted him with the double bind he placed on his managers by asking them to first and foremost focus on the company as a whole, only to exclusively work with individual departments and criticize the managers if their department wasn't performing perfectly. In the beginning, Eric felt that it was necessary that the managers could both act on behalf of the company and represent their individual departments. I agreed with this, but explained to him that the managers did not experience this. Instead, the managers felt trapped by having to trust that it paid to focus on the business first, while Eric's behavior indicated that they should focus on their own department first. Eric and I agreed to discuss this at the next senior management group meeting.

The second element arose at the meeting, when Eric said that he had been feeling frustrated that the group wasn't able to think strategically together, but that he had realized that he wasn't actually challenging them to do so. The managers agreed with him, and each of them said that they hadn't been able to focus on the company when they were unsure if they would be "excluded" if they said something that Eric didn't agree with.

This led to a good discussion about how the managers knew that they had to contribute to strategic thinking among the senior management group on the one hand, but that they had to perform well individually on the other hand. This paradox of belonging resembles one of Lego's paradoxes of needing to first focus on the individual department *and* work loyally for the company as a whole. The senior manager agreed that it was important to talk about this balancing act in the group's meetings so that they could continually focus on both alternatives. In addition, Eric would include more problems that related to the individual departments on the agenda, so that the group could work together to create an oversight and a feeling of coherence. The idea was that discussing the various departments would allow the individual manager to feel that decisions (for example, that the service manager should transfer assignments to the project-sales department) were clear and agreed-upon, rather than being an expression of a lack of performance. This clarity would allow the senior management group to achieve workable certainty.

This discussion led to yet another paradox. During the meeting, one of the managers said: "Eric, you need to realize that you have asked us to discuss, challenge, and disrupt your thoughts and give our opinions on things. But at the same time, you come down on us hard if we don't completely agree with what you want. So we have to be obedient and disobedient at the same time! That can be difficult. So we choose to shelve our opinions and do what creates the fewest problems. We know that we hold our cards too close, but it's just what is least dangerous!"

Eric understood that he needed to create more of a cohesive management group and reduce the system of rewards/punishments in individual departments in order to achieve a shared perspective. In addition, the managers understood that they needed to make their thoughts, objections, etc. more visible, and that it was just as dangerous to keep quiet. We discussed the paradox of autonomy: You are asked to be disobedient – so to be obedient you have to be disobedient – in other words, you have to challenge Eric's decisions. You are also obedient if you dare to be "disobedient" – while at the same time, you need to manage your department in relation to the strategic decisions that have been made.

The Unimotor example illustrates how good leadership means, among other things, the courage to address the ambivalence that arises when a manager is both part of a group (centralized focus) and simultaneously responsible for his or her department (decentralized focus). The organizational paradox of centralized–decentralized focus is part of the organization that allows managers to both be responsible for elements of the company and be able to deprioritize their individual departments when necessary. It is only through discussing these double affiliations and the corresponding ambivalence that senior management can collaborate in order to negotiate the delicate balance between trust in the group and maintaining individual security through "staying on dry land." Trust in management groups can only be built through these types of conversations. In addition, these conversations are essential for being able to manage both elements in the organizational paradox between centralization and decentralization.

I find that paradoxes of belonging are especially difficult to negotiate. Often managers are not accustomed to talking about the more "personal experiences" that are attached to the paradoxes of leadership. However, as the examples in this chapter show, it is essential for the company's performance level that the more personal experiences are also taken into account. My claim is that they are often one of the completely essential parameters that determine if a strategy succeeds. Ambivalence can lead to paralysis and the inability to act, or, as a worst-case scenario, that employees and managers say one thing and do another. It is this element that cannot be managed through new strategic approaches, or through recruitment alone, or even through tighter control. It can only be managed through a forum where the ambivalence caused by organizational complexity can be shared, confronted, and managed, in order to reach a balancing point of trust.

Therefore, managers must be aware of the double binds that can be created by their own insecurities or ambivalence. In the Unimotor example, double binds were created by Eric's communication when he announced that managers should prioritize thinking about the company as a whole, but his behavior focused on individual departments. The situation was worsened when he then criticized his managers for not understanding his message regarding transparency and shared focus. It was only when Eric became aware of this ambiguous communication that he was able to set it on the agenda for discussion, and then work to break the double binds. This allowed for a progression from a double bind to a shared ambivalence that could be dealt with through collaboration within the senior management team.

Double binds and ambivalence are difficult to access. Managers need to be able to transform doubt into a "reflective companion." They need to be able to catch themselves when they communicate ambiguously, or when they say one thing and do something else. In addition, managers must have the courage to examine where their own ambivalence comes from and why they are communicating ambiguously. Managers cannot avoid occasionally communicating in double binds, but it is essential that they examine their own motives so that the ambivalence can be shared with the group. For example, Eric had to confront the fact that while he expressed trust that his management group could run their departments and be loyal to the entirety of the company, his actions demonstrated control in order to ensure that each manager did what he said and delivered acceptable performance.

Here is another narrative that involves the paradox of belonging:

The autonomy paradox

> While consulting with Carletti, I worked with the creation of a process of cultural change that should allow employees to have more ownership of problems related to production. The idea was that they would take responsibility for the organization, correcting mistakes in production, and finding creative solutions for launching new products. Until that point, management had closely monitored the employees, and when things didn't go according to plan, management took over and corrected mistakes or found their own solutions. We worked with the autonomy paradox: "Make an autonomous decision!" (and I'm the one who defines what is 'autonomous'). When management continually took control, they confirmed the employees' feelings that they weren't autonomous after all.
>
> In a brainstorming session with the director, we discussed the situation and concluded that he needed to stop taking over when his managers didn't do things exactly the way he would have done them. The director had to confront the ambivalence he felt by insisting on autonomous employees. On the one hand, he wanted to have managers who took initiative, but on the other hand, he found it difficult not to intervene when the managers made a different decision than the one he would have made. He constantly said, "Can't they just make an autonomous decision?" However, this was exactly what they had done, they just weren't able to independently evaluate if it was the correct decision.

The director in this example needed to learn to "sit on his hands" and create some guidelines for solving the assignment, but avoid solving the problem by himself. Then, if the managers didn't live up to the agreement, he could either insist that they redid the assignment, or he could brainstorm with them in order to train them to make decisions that matched the shared strategy of the company. However, this could only be accomplished if the director confronted his own ambivalence. This confrontation would allow him to work on acting more clearly, as well as being able to discuss when employees should increase or decrease their autonomy. The paradox of belonging needed to be addressed so that the director could avoid his dependency on managers while simultaneously insisting that they be autonomous.

The paradox of belonging: propriety–honesty

A manager at Lego needed to have a meeting with his team. There was tension in the air because two employees thought that they were doing all of the work in the team. The manager opened the meeting by saying, "Now we need to have an honest conversation where we can politely discuss this." However, the problem was that if the employees had to be honest, they might not have so many polite things to say. The employees couldn't be both honest and polite, and so they remained silent…

During a brainstorming session, the Lego manager realized that he had been communicating ambiguously because of his own ambivalence. On the one hand, he wanted to work with the conflict to solve it. But on the other hand, he couldn't stand it when the conversation became negative, and felt uncomfortable when the employees spoke harshly to one another. He was ambivalent about solving the conflict. By recognizing this ambivalence and ambiguity (let's solve the conflict = communicate honestly, versus, let's avoid conflict = let's be polite), he was able to see that he had communicated his own desire to solve the conflict without really working with it.

This resulted in the manager separating the ideas of honesty and propriety. "Let's be honest about what you experience," he said, "so that we can understand each other and start being polite to one another."

There are many more examples of how paradoxes of belonging are in danger of directing much of management's communication. Paradoxes of belonging are necessary so that communication can become a clearer recognition of what each manager has invested in relationships. Notice that discussing a paradox does not eliminate it, but makes it part of the organizational reality. In each organization there is pressure resulting from the various affiliations of each manager. These affiliations are communicated through double binds and contradictory messages.

Although I often experience that paradoxes of belonging are the most difficult type of paradox to work with, it is also my experience that managers who work with the personal aspects of their organizational communication are able to handle the pressure between the whole and individual elements, trust and control, professionalism and the bottom line, creativity and business, etc. The ambivalence that is connected with these pressures can be communicated more clearly when they are shared within the organization. This is not done through reducing complexity, but through managing complexity and being able to operate within the psychological complexity that is related to the process of change within the organization.

Summary

Throughout Chapters 4–9, we have seen how we can work with various leadership paradoxes. The organizational paradoxes can be discussed using the Competing Values Framework model, and management groups can use the model to create a *strategic leadership action plan* in order to create balance in the paradoxes of relationships–results and change–stability.

We could identify many more organizational paradoxes, but the CVF model provides a starting point for thinking about managing complexity and double focus, while working with strategic organizational development.

The role paradoxes are varied, and set complex and contradictory demands for managers. In this case, the CVF model allows management groups to discuss how they should adjust their leadership in order to accommodate the strategic areas that have been established in the organization. There are also many role paradoxes that were illustrated by the Lego example. Using the Lego example, we saw how the quadrant model can be used in order to identify relevant paradoxes for individual managers. Leadership always originates from a role (or position). You can use paradoxical thinking in order to determine which position you should use to lead your organization, as well as which questions you should ask yourself.

The paradoxes of belonging, which we have explored in this chapter, are the most difficult type of paradox for two reasons. First, they deal with the more emotional aspects of organizational life. Second, these paradoxes are often hidden and unnoticed, since managers communicate double binds to their employees and each other. These double binds are difficult to discuss, but it is necessary to do so in order to create clarity and workable certainty for managers and employees. This is essential so that they can and will *confront their own ambivalence*, contradictions, and double binds in order to create shared meaning during organizational change.

It can be helpful for you to work with the questions below in order to gain access to the paradoxes of belonging:

REFLECTION: PARADOX OF BELONGING IN PRACTICE

1. What type of organizational pressure am I currently feeling (i.e. between the political and operational level, or between shareholder interests and professionalism)?
2. How does this affect my decisions?

3. How can I discuss this pressure with my management/board of directors/shareholders in a way that ensures that I remain visible, but also allows them to take complexity into account?
4. How much do I trust my own management group?
5. What kind of courage do I need to have in order to share the ambivalence that I am experiencing?
6. What do I hope will result from discussing this ambivalence?
7. Which brave step do I need to take in order to achieve this result?
8. What do I think will happen to the group dynamic if we can collectively manage these paradoxes?

The narratives in this chapter have demonstrated how these questions become a part of the leadership development in the organization, and the management group can navigate complexity. Complex problems can only be addressed through complex methods of relating to one another. Cross-pressure, ambivalence, and double binds are part of the paradoxes of belonging, and these elements can only become manageable and clear through dialogue and shared reflection.

I have now presented you with a complex leadership concept. In the third part of the book we will examine what it means to deal with paradoxes. How can you lead through paradox? Part III examines how to retain the ability to act when relating to complexity and paradoxes on all organizational levels.

PART III

Leading through paradox
Acceptance, positioning, and integrative thinking

10
INTEGRATIVE THINKING

In the literature, management is often presented as a multifaceted discipline. In an article about leadership, "Leadership that gets results," Goleman (2000) presents a list of leadership qualities that are central to determining whether an organization succeeds or fails. His point is that managers should draw on at least four of the six different leadership qualities: authoritative, affiliative (focused on relationships), democratic, pacesetting, coaching, and coercive. Goleman claims that managers who can read employees' needs, and who can listen and identify those needs, are the managers who will be most successful in creating employee well-being and results (Goleman, 2000). He calls this ability social intelligence. He warns against using the pacesetting and coaching leadership styles, since these styles have a direct negative influence on employee well-being and results. At the same time, he claims that a narrower use of these leadership styles can sometimes be temporarily necessary, but should never be used as a permanent leadership style.

But what is the point of Goleman's different leadership styles? Is it that managers should possess all of these qualities in order to be a good leader? Or is his point that we all have an ability to demonstrate these leadership styles and that we need to shift between them?

Goleman's research regarding social intelligence shows that managers need to use their social intelligence in order to read their employees and their needs. He claims that managers can develop their social intelligence through practice, and therefore become better at identifying which leadership style is required in any given situation. He uses a golf bag as a metaphor for the repertoire of leadership positions available to a manager. If the manager has a golf bag with many different golf clubs, he or she will be able to select the club that is best suited to the problem at hand. The landscape, the ball, placement, and the goal are all taken into consideration so that the manager is able to select the golf club that will best match the situation. This choice is based on the club that will give the manager the best chance to achieve his or her goal.

To a great extent, Goleman makes an important point when he states that good leadership is about having a wide repertoire of options. However, he neglects one important leadership quality: what could be called strategic or organizational intelligence. As we have seen in earlier chapters, a manager must be able to read employees' needs, but he or she must also be able to connect those needs to the needs of the organization. The needs experienced by the employees and management are not always the same. It is the manager's task to connect the internal approach with the external demands or opportunities as well as the results that the organization needs to achieve.

For example, if a manager needs to create a growth strategy, he or she needs to evaluate the needs of the employees in regard to the strategy and be able to ask the question, "What is needed in order to create a foundation for this type of growth?" In Chapter 4, we saw how organizational paradoxes led to questions regarding where the organization's focus should be (in the CVF model) in regard to the vision and/or goals of the company.

Goleman focuses more on the relationship aspects of leadership than he does on the strategic aspects. In other words, this is a focus with which managers look only at the relationship-oriented aspects of the leadership role. If managers use only social intelligence, they will adjust their leadership approach toward the emotional needs of their employees. This could be, for example, to avoid too much disruption by avoiding too many changes. This type of situation could arise if an organization is in the midst of a large turnaround in order to survive or grow. In this case, the employees' need for stability must be considered in relation to the demands for change from senior management, and managers must ask themselves: How can we create appropriate stability and calm so that the employees can find the energy to accomplish these extensive changes? This question can be followed by another: Where do we need to create calm so that we can have a surplus of energy to devote to change? In other words, the manager must both relate to the employees and the need for the organization to develop and use this information in order to create workable certainty so that he or she can lead.

As I have already stated, it is these contradictory and complex demands that constantly arise in the leadership discipline. Many managers have learned to make decisions using "either-or" choices and evaluations. For example: We can either create stable growth or we can invest in something that is bigger and better. We can either serve our own shareholders or we can serve the environment (where these interests are contradictory). We can either serve the interests of our employees or we can serve the interests of capital. But what if there was a way where we could serve both of these contradictory interests simultaneously? What if we could create growth and atmosphere at the same time? What if we could create innovation as well as maintain the core values of the company? What if we could see well-being and efficiency as preconditions for one another? The organizational paradoxes in the CVF model show how relationships (the human element) can be considered alongside the more goal-oriented, "bottom-line" aspects (results).

What does "organizational intelligence" mean in this situation? It means that we must both have social emotional intelligence and be able to examine how we can understand organizational problems. When we view a paradox as a mental construction (a way of understanding complex problems), we must realize that it is necessary to accommodate the paradox when thinking of possible solutions.

In this chapter and the next two chapters, I will explain three different ways of relating to paradoxes. The three methods are:

1. Integrative thinking (in this chapter).
2. Reflective distance and positioning – the ability to occupy different positions at different times in order to balance the alternatives of the paradox (Chapter 11).
3. Acceptance of the complexity – understanding that this is a fundamental premise for organizational change (Chapter 12).

All three methods use paradoxes in their approaches. We will begin by examining integrative thinking as an approach to organizational paradoxes, role paradoxes, and paradoxes of belonging.

Leading through integrative thinking

Integrative thinking is an important skill for managing the complex problems that arise in an organization. Integrative thinking means finding solutions through including the contradictory elements of our thought processes. These contradictory thoughts can seem to be mutually exclusive at first, but they must both be a part of the final solution. In other words, a solution is not finding a choice *between* contradictions, but rather a choice *within* contradiction.

Integrative thinking is, in itself, a creative ability. Creativity lies in the ability to constructively manage contradictory ideas, rather than choosing one idea at the cost of another. It is the ability to generate a creative solution that contains elements from both ideas. For example, in relation to the question of how much leadership development should be centralized or decentralized in an organization, integrative thinking means finding a way to include both needs. This can be done in various ways. The following section will provide examples of how to use integrative thinking.

Vision Tech

The following example is my interpretation of a case from the book, *The Opposable Mind* (Martin, 2007), which illustrates how apparently incompatible sets of logic can be brought together to create a paradoxical solution.

> Sally and Bill are two directors from a company called Vision Tech. Just like everyone else, they form opinions based on the information that surrounds them, and, just like all of us, they have a tendency to believe that their own opinions are reality.

Sally and Bill have just returned from meeting with an important client. During the meeting, the client said, "I really like Vision Tech. You have led the market in terms of innovation for a long time. But I am under rising financial pressure, and I have to prioritize."

This statement from the client is just a statement, but we unconsciously give it meaning, and what that meaning is varies from person to person. Sally zoomed in on the first two sentences ("I really like Vision Tech. You have led the market in terms of innovation for a long time.") She didn't assign the rest of the sentence much meaning or importance ("But I am under rising financial pressure, and I have to prioritize"). She felt that her recollection was correct. And it is true that the words came out of the client's mouth in the order she remembered. However, because she didn't catch the rest of the client's statement, she didn't give it much meaning. In her understanding, the client told them how much he appreciated Vision Tech's leadership and innovation.

In addition, "really like" and "appreciate" are two different concepts. Sally concluded that "really like" meant that the client was willing to pay for the way Vision Tech had chosen to compete in the market. Therefore, Sally's conclusion based on the meeting was confirming and calming. According to her conclusion, the client appreciated that Vision Tech would continue to work with innovation and leadership in order to create results.

On the other hand, Bill was immediately much more concerned. He had heard the complimenting words as a friendly introduction to the client's true statement, that Vision Tech was too expensive because the client was under financial pressure. Bill had heard the message as: "But I am under rising financial pressure, and I have to prioritize."

Bill concluded that Vision Tech was at risk of losing a client because its prices and costs were too high for the client. His conclusion was that Vision Tech needed to try to reduce costs in order to be more competitive in regard to prices.

The two managers then discussed strategy. Sally thought, "Didn't Bill hear what our client appreciates and chooses us for? Or does he have a hidden agenda which is making him ignore the client and cut costs, which is actually the opposite of what the client wants?" But she says, "But Bill, our customer expects that we continue to be first within leadership and innovation!"

Bill can't believe his own ears: "Was Sally not there at the meeting? Or does she have a hidden agenda which is making her completely ignore the client's wishes and demands on cost reduction, and she just wants to keep going with innovation, even when it's too expensive? That's exactly the opposite of what the client wants!"

Within research regarding recognition processes, it is a common assumption that humans believe that what we see is what really happened. This belief makes it difficult for us to hear what the other person is actually saying, and we quickly focus on determining who is right and who is wrong. In other words, we need to know who is best at reflecting what "really" happened. Therefore, we begin to argue that one of us has to be right. However, when we reject the other person's model of the world, we miss out on the development opportunity that lies in working within the contradictory models. We have a tendency to ignore our ability to manage complexity even before it could help us find a creative solution.

Integrative thinking is being able to avoid taking sides regarding the two opinions, and instead focusing on finding solutions that contain both sides of the paradox. If we look at the Vision Tech example of the "high quality–low budget" paradox, we can see that both sides are both wrong when taken individually. While the problem first appears to be a dilemma between solving the crisis either through leadership and innovation or through reducing costs and prices, either solution will in fact end with the company losing a client. The art is in being able to combine the two understandings of the problem and increase the quality of the solution so that it can contain both understandings.

The Vision Tech example shows that two completely different sets of logic can be applied to the same problem, which in turn leads to two completely contradictory patterns of action. The art of paradoxical thinking is to merge these two sets of logic and relate to both when determining the leadership approach. But how does a manager do that?[1]

There are many different ways to relate to a paradox. You can either create a kind of synthesis and include the paradox in the new solution, or confront your contradictory feelings and accept that the paradox is part of a manager's recognition process. The solution that benefits the company is most likely the one that points toward synergy or integrative thinking. This means engaging in an innovative process where the problem is "reframed" so that it contains the contradictory sets of logic. In relation to the example above, the solution could be that Sally and Bill create a marketing strategy that includes both the aspects that the client likes *and* the aspects where the client needs to cut costs. Perhaps they could develop a product that is both cost-saving for the client *and* innovative and appropriate to the individual needs of the client.

The path to synthesis is typically found where there is external pressure. In other words, this path is found where there is pressure to rethink sales, performance, or product in order to maintain the company's place in the market. In the Vision Tech example, the change–stability paradox is ideally suited for innovative thinking.

In the example from the Lego project, we saw how organizational paradoxes called for integrative thinking between change and stability. Senior management tried to both hold on to the Jutland spirit, Lego blocks, and simple construction play as a central product, and create strategic international alliances, high-tech construction (i.e. Lego Mindstorms), and increased globalized thinking. Both aspects were on the agenda. The products and the strategic approach reflected integrative thinking. Both change-related values and stability-related values were integrated into a solution.

Here is another example from an international corporation where I worked with the HR department in order to help them reach a decision regarding their manager training program in the global market:

> The management of a large company needed to develop a training program for all of the managers within the corporation. I used the dialogue model (as we saw in Chapter 3) in order to move the HR manager group toward paradoxical thinking regarding possible alternatives. The phases of the model are: formulating the problem, the dilemma, the paradox, and workable certainty. The sessions looked like this:
>
> In the first part of the process (formulating the problem), we attempted to sharpen the description of the problem that was inherent in the question of whether to centralize or decentralize manager training. The question was: How should we approach manager training within the corporation?
>
> When we continued to discuss the problem, a question arose which was then formulated as a dilemma: The dilemma of to what degree the company should centralize manager training so that it would be approved by Corporate HR. This would allow for uniformity within the management discipline (but the departments would not be able to have influence over the process in order to adjust it to meet the needs of their own work culture and methods). Alternatively, the manager training could be decentralized, so that it was adjusted to fit the individual department culture (but the company would not be able to evaluate and place managers to the same international standards as before). Among other things, this would mean that it would become difficult to discuss what managers needed to demonstrate in order to be promoted or transferred to a particular position, because the required skills could be completely different. A certain degree of uniformity was required within manager development.
>
> Herein lies the dilemma. If we remained on this level in the dialogue, the answer would be one solution at the cost of the other. It would be an "either-or" solution. The progression from dilemma to solution therefore required that we delve into the logic behind each solution. When solutions are formulated as a dilemma (a choice with significant consequences), it can be useful to work with the logic behind each solution and evaluate it based on what each would require. However, how do you move toward an integrative solution and create a solution that encompasses both ends of the paradox? At Lego, I discovered that one option was to map out the requirements of both positions.
>
> I asked the following questions:

1. What advantages are there in one solution as opposed to the other?
2. What will each solution provide to the organization?
3. Where is the central value of the company reflected within each solution?
4. What are the requirements of making the centralizing logic the definitive solution to the question of manager training within the organization?

The final question is important because it is here where managers experience that this type of logic has some limitations, which means that it cannot define the entire solution. For example, centralizing would demand that all of the local units had more or less the same type of organization and managerial titles/hierarchy. All of the local units needed to be able to be incorporated in Corporate HR, and this would require that a manager training program could be developed that allowed HR to be familiar with the local relationships. Corporate HR would also require that some key people were willing to take ownership of the model that was presented.

There were similar conditions for the logic behind decentralizing the manager training, which showed that it wasn't the best answer to the problem either. One obvious limitation was that if the training was decentralized, many resources would be needed to adjust and develop the concept, as well as to ensure that the training was compatible with the approach taken in other departments. This would ensure that managers could be transferred to different regions and still have a good chance at managing in accordance with the guidelines of the organization as a whole. In order for this to succeed, the local departments would have to be in close contact with the central HR.

It is worth taking the time to consider the limitations that are connected to each solution. A closer examination of these limitations will create an increasing need to find solutions that include both sets of logic, and yet still maintain the advantages of each idea. Here we found that the dialogue was nearing a paradox: participants began to discuss how the features and culture of decentralized training could be included in a shared model. For example, could they create a central framework that would allow departments in different countries to design a manager development program that lived up to the central demands of uniformity? What could be done in collaboration so that it was possible for managers to be transferred and/or promoted between organizational locations?

In this example, an integrative solution was found when HR developed some unified training platforms in the form of models. This provided some guidelines that applied throughout the corporation, and served as a collective framework for manager training in all departments. At the same time, it allowed local departments to adjust the concept to their own organization, leadership culture, and needs.

Although this solution appears to be very simple once it was discovered, it still includes elements of both apparently exclusive solutions. This exercise shows how to create workable certainty by actively considering the advantages and disadvantages of each alternative. This allows the solution to be more than a simple compromise, but instead a solution that contains the elements that were important to the success of the manager training program.

Many meetings follow this pattern, but in many of the organizations I work with, I see that there is often an argument between alternatives, where one of the two alternatives must "win" in order to find a solution — as if it was a simple problem with one matching solution. If a manager wants to appear to be friendly and not offend his or her opponents, he or she must compromise and allow the opposition to work alternative elements into the solution. Working with integrative thinking allows managers to work through the problem more thoroughly and discover a solution which retains complexity. The advantage of this method is that those who hold on to one way of thinking are forced to rethink and find the conditions and limitations that exist within their own model. By engaging in this process, they are able to see the need for integrative thinking and therefore find a creative way forward.

Summary

Integrative thinking is a way of managing complexity within organizational problems. This requires that managers are willing to include paradoxes and requires that they must practice some reflective processes, which will allow them to reach workable certainty.

REFLECTION: THINKING IN A WAY THAT INCLUDES PARADOXES

1. Formulate the problem (How do we train the leaders within the entire corporation?)
2. Which alternatives do we have? (The dilemma: Should we centralize or decentralize the manager training program?)
3. Which problems will each alternative answer?
4. For each alternative: What are the requirements for choosing this solution?
5. For each alternative: What limitations are there in this solution?
6. What should the solution be able to accomplish? (What should remain decentralized, what should centralization accomplish?)
7. What solution can we create that will include these elements? What type of metaphor or image describes this solution? (Centralized templates with decentralized options for adjustment. In this case we used the image of an IT platform as a shared platform with options for individual adjustments as needed.)

Integrative thinking arises when managers begin to manage complexity and simultaneously account for contradictory demands. This allows them to move from "either-or" thinking to "both-and" thinking. In Chapter 2, I presented two leadership paradigms: the modern and the postmodern. Integrative thinking is comparable to what was explained in Chapter 2 as the paradigm bridge: Leadership means thinking in terms of modern boundary keeping, setting guidelines, showing direction, and setting goals. However, leadership must also create space for employees to have influence, collaborate, and be involved. Both of these perspectives must be maintained when facing a concrete problem. In the above example, the company that was attempting to centralize and decentralize at the same time was able to create an integration of two paradigms, and therefore find a solution that included both the need to show global direction *and* the need for the solution to be locally created by each individual management group.

Integrative thinking means that you are able to question your own solutions, but also to go a step farther and question your own understanding of these solutions. When integrative thinking is connected with organizational intelligence, it allows managers to connect the organization's strategy with the needs of the employees. These two elements sometimes contain contradictory values, but each element is still dependent on the other.

Note

1 In the traditional competition strategy method of thinking, we would say (according to Michael Porter) that you can either choose cost reduction *or* market differentiation. If you don't do that, you will be unavoidably trapped between the two strategies and not succeed in either of them. Integrative thinking disagrees with this thought process, since cost reduction and market differentiation should be thought of as going hand-in-hand as much as possible. This allows for a creative and competitive connection between the strategies.

11

REFLECTIVE DISTANCE, OSCILLATION, AND POSITIONING

In the previous chapter, we investigated the need for managers to be able to think in complex terms and integrate contradictory challenges in a reflection process that matches the complexity of the organization. I identified organizational intelligence as a reflective requirement for being able to include both alternatives when working with a paradoxical problem. I often find that management groups are encouraged to treat conflicting interests as one alternative against another in order to find effective solutions. However, the paradox does not disappear just because you choose a side. Indeed, choosing one alternative just increases the pressure from the other alternative. For example, if you choose to practice an involved and supportive leadership style, you will find that the need for visible leadership, guidelines, and direction will become stronger. You will always have to turn your back on something, but it will still be there nonetheless.

In this kind of situation, it can be helpful to be able to use integrative thinking. Important questions to ask yourself and the management group are: Which elements from the alternatives are important to consider in order to make a decision? How do we include complexity in a collective "here and now" solution? Which elements are represented by various employees or managers? How can these apparently contradictory points of view be brought together and combined in new ways?

However, having an integrative thinking approach is not always sufficient. Integrative thinking allows you to avoid falling into the "oversimplification" trap, where only one of the alternatives is represented in the solution. However, the thought alone is not enough. Action is required. The question is, how can you relate to the paradox using action instead of words?

Integrative thinking focuses on formulating the problem so that you can include elements from the seemingly exclusive alternatives. The theory of competing values invites you to act using reflective distance and positioning in order to manage the paradox.

In this chapter, I will begin by presenting a reflection model that can help you determine which role paradox is most relevant to you. The model provides a guideline for you to be able to see which positions you take in the paradox, which are most desirable, and which are less desirable. You will then be able to see how reflective distance and the ability to occupy different positions within the paradox are necessary for your leadership practice. The chapter ends with some reflective questions for your own leadership practice and oscillation within the role paradoxes.

Personal tendencies and preferences within paradoxes

Leadership does not exist in a vacuum; that is to say that our values, upbringing, self-understanding, and personality affect our tendencies to position ourselves within the paradoxes of leadership. In Chapter 2, I described the postmodern and modern paradigms. Most managers have a tendency to primarily think about leadership and act using only one of the paradigms as their reference point.

When it comes to the many paradoxes of leadership that we encounter, our choices are often affected by our personal preferences as well as the popular discourse regarding the definition of good management. Personality tests and profiles are often used in order to identify our personal approach to leadership and our leadership preferences, but they also shed light on our own blind spots regarding leadership.

JTI, MBTI, Neo-Pi-r, ADIZE, Belbin, Discover, and many other tests measure our personal leadership in order to help us be more aware of what we tend to focus on in our leadership practice. There is nothing wrong with that approach, but, in a postmodern perspective, it is difficult to operate with something that focuses on detecting stable patterns of who you "are." Of course we recognize that most managers have a preferred leadership style, or what could be called a managerial "right leg" (the leg you prefer to use to shoot with in soccer). It is possible to claim that your preferred leadership style is relatively stable, and that it is one of the "skills" that you will most often identify when asked to name something you are good at, feel comfortable with, and feel is relatively easy to accomplish.

However, if we think in terms of role paradoxes, we can also identify the opposite pole of this "leadership skill" as being a necessary leadership position to use in your management practice. We could call this pole the "left leg" (the leg you shoot poorly with, but have to use sometimes anyway). This leadership style might not be your preferred style because it isn't as accessible, or because it is associated with insecurity or unease.

Although you have a preferred leadership style, you still have to be able to draw on the other leadership styles that aren't as comfortable or natural. However, in contrast to the tests and profiles above, the paradox view calls for thinking in terms of positioning yourself in the paradox rather than identifying strengths and preferred positions. In accordance with paradoxical thinking, you need to be a "corporate athlete." In other words, you need to be able to oscillate between positions within role paradoxes and avoid relying on being a certain "kind of leader." Now, what is so important about this point?

The paradoxical message is that even though you have something that is easier for you, leadership based on paradoxical thinking means taking the position that is most useful in order to support an organizational need, rather than choosing the position that is your preferred personal style. In other words, it is important to be able to identify which positions you find easy to take on and which positions you have a tendency to downplay or find difficult, even in those situations where those positions are necessary. In addition, in Chapter 2, we saw how the leadership paradigms contain norms and discourses that are popular within the culture of an organization and can easily be taken for granted. For example, I have been a consultant in many organizations where the trust–control paradox is especially relevant. Managers have some of the postmodern assumptions that trust is good, but they find it difficult to ensure that things run smoothly because a sense of control is not included in their understanding of good leadership. As we have seen in the paradoxes of belonging, it is problematic when managers cannot discuss both sides of paradoxes, because they continue to exist even when ignored. Control sneaks in in the form of demands for documentation, employee-developmental conversations, time registration, report systems, etc. Therefore, it becomes evident that trust isn't absolute, and it is important to be able to talk about control.

Both sides of the paradox are important in relation to being able to place the needs of the organization on the agenda rather than choosing to focus on personal leadership preferences or the preferred leadership paradigm of the organization. Another advantage is that it will be easier to be able to challenge yourself to take on non-preferred positions when required, and you will also be able to enjoy identifying the situations in which you need to be able to occupy different positions.

In collaboration with a colleague, I have developed an exercise that can be used in connection with leadership development. We call it the paradox exercise, and it provides managers with the opportunity to use their preferred/non-preferred leadership positions in order to evaluate which leadership values are important to balance, as well as which position is easiest to occupy.

The paradox exercise

1. Find a positive leadership position that you can easily occupy

Find a piece of paper and draw a square (10 cm × 10 cm). Divide the square into four quadrants as shown in Table 11.1.

Write a positive leadership position (i.e. "involving") in the top-left quadrant. This position should be one that highlights you as a manager and one that you know your employees, colleagues, and managers appreciate about you.

TABLE 11.1 The paradox exercise

Write a positive leadership quality about yourself here

TABLE 11.2 The paradox exercise: prominent leadership qualities

Write a positive leadership quality about yourself here (involving)	Write what the leadership quality is called when it becomes too much of a good thing

2. Pitfalls – when it's too much of a good thing

Imagine that the leadership position you have written in the top-left quadrant is over-used; that you draw on it in too many situations. What is the position called when it is "too much of a good thing," i.e. when the position is over-done? Write the name of this characteristic in the top-right corner of the quadrant. (For example, when "involving" is over-used, you can call it "indecisive/invisible"; see Table 11.2.)

3. The positive opposite

If you over-use the leadership position you have identified in the top-right quadrant, you need to change positions. Think in terms of positioning within the paradox and write "the positive opposite" of this leadership behavior in the bottom-right corner. In other words, this is the opposite of the leadership quality that can be "too much of a good thing." Write your description in the bottom-right quadrant. (For example, if you become "invisible," you would write "directive".)

4. The positive opposite – but too much of a good thing

The leadership behavior that you have just written in the bottom-right quadrant is a behavior that is sometimes useful to pursue in your leadership practice. Now, imagine that this behavior is over-used; you used too much of the behavior in the bottom-right quadrant, and it became "too much of a good thing." What would it be called? Write this in the bottom-left quadrant. (For example, too much "directive" behavior would be "dictatorship".)

Now there is a prominent leadership paradox in the top-left quadrant and bottom-right quadrant. This paradox will be useful for you to focus on throughout your leadership practice. The paradox in this example is involving/directive. The side of the paradox in quadrant one is the preferred position (involving), and the second is the leadership position that is worth reflecting on. In which situations

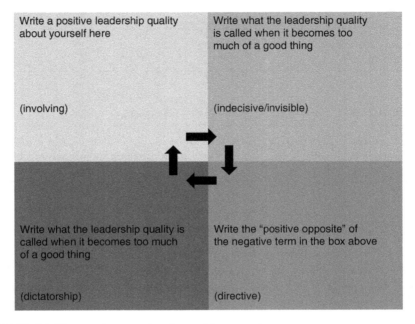

FIGURE 11.1 The paradox exercise: the positive opposite

is it important for you to also lead from that position? The paradox is shown in Figure 11.1.

The pitfalls

As the example in Figure 11.1 shows, it is important to relate to the pitfalls that are found in your preferred leadership style. The pitfall in an involving leadership style (top left) is that it can be over-used, simply because it is well-known, effective, feels right, and complies with your basic values or popular discourse about good leadership. The pitfall that is worth paying attention to (top right) is the over-use of this leadership behavior. In which situations do you have a tendency to over-use your preferred leadership style? In which situations should you therefore stop and ask yourself if that style will be effective in order to achieve in the organization/in relation to concrete tasks? Here you will find that doubt will help you, and in order to optimize your leadership practice you will have to question how well your leadership behavior matches the given situation. It can be a good idea to ask yourself the following questions:

- In which situations can I see that my preferred leadership style is especially useful and is a strength?
- What are the advantages of having such a strong preference for this position?
- In which situations has this leadership behavior failed me? Where can I see that it isn't effective?

- In which situations can I see that it would have been better to occupy the opposite position?
- What would have been the result if I had chosen the opposite position?

The last question is important in order to identify the situations where it could have been beneficial to switch to the behavior you have a tendency to "turn your back on," but where you avoided doing so because you didn't feel it was as familiar/comfortable/safe/popular as your preferred behavior.

Fear

The bottom-right quadrant shows where it will be advantageous for you to challenge yourself in regard to your leadership reflection. In which situations would it have been beneficial to occupy the alternative in your leadership paradox? What stopped you? A common answer is that you were afraid of ending up in the bottom-left quadrant, where the leadership behavior would be over-used. As a rule, it is this position that is closer to the values that we don't like so much. Therefore, it becomes our managerial "left leg." Our left leg is the leadership behavior that we tend to avoid because something else is more familiar and safe. Therefore, you should ask yourself the following questions:

- Where would I be worried about ending up if I used this behavior more?
- Which leaders can I identify who have used/been exposed to the leadership behavior I have tried to avoid?
- Which experiences do I have (from my leadership practice or elsewhere) where there has been too much of a good thing and I have ended up in the bottom-left quadrant? How can I avoid ending up there again?

Fear is what gets in the way of being able to choose your position freely within paradoxes. Therefore, it is important that you relate to the challenge, as well as to how you can find an appropriate balance within the paradox so that you can avoid ending up in extremes. Extremes result in the paradox being experienced as negative.

The result of the paradox exercise is that it shows a preferred paradox. The directive–involving example is shown in Figure 11.2.

Reflective distance

I work with management groups that are made up of managers from very different companies and branches. One of the strengths of these groups is that they can use their different company cultures and different experience to influence one another, and effectively disrupt the habitual way of thinking that managers have in connection with their individual problems. For example, a director from a private company can think in terms of profiling and market orientation when a manager

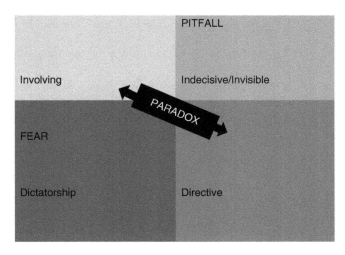

FIGURE 11.2 The paradox exercise: too much of the opposite

from a public institution needs to expand his or her services to additional counties or citizens. The manager from the public institution can then offer the private director good conversation models for team development, etc. A manager who tends to think that he has recruited the wrong people could be helped to see the potential for development within those employees. This allows the managers to receive constructive feedback regarding their own leadership practices. This is another way to create reflection within your leadership – to let your reflections be "tested" and qualified by a group of managers who have an outsider perspective.

I create this type of group based on the need for reflective distance. Paradoxical thinking allows managers to have the space and opportunity to think about their business and their leadership. Good leadership is essential for an organization's success. However, managers often don't think about leadership as their core responsibility, nor do they consider what is reflected in their leadership behavior. As a manager, your primary responsibility is to lead your employees by using the perspective that is most useful when helping the organization or department move toward the chosen strategy. You must create a connection between the employees and the goal. In addition, as we have seen in the CVF model in Chapters 4–7, this must be done differently depending on the challenges facing the company, as well as the composition of the employee group, etc. Reflective distance means taking a step away from the goal of the day and the current problem in order to spend time reflecting on which type of leadership is needed in the organization at the moment. It is important that both the individual manager and the management group as a whole are able to reflect over the leadership task and conduct leadership as a collective concern and a shared reflective practice.

Individual leadership development can take place through individual reflection and preparation, but it can also be especially beneficial to meet with other managers

Strategy

- Vision
- Goal
- Strategy
- Structure
- Organization

Answer the questions:
1. Where do we want to go?
2. Which areas need our attention in the near future?
3. Which leadership focus will support this? (organizational paradoxes and the CVF model)

Leadership

- Prioritizing
- Communication
- Personnel leadership
- Involvement
- Leadership initiatives

Answer the questions:
1. What is the status of the organization?
2. Which leadership initiatives do we need to take regarding our strategy (based on operational status)
3. What does this mean we need to do as managers (and when working together with the employees)?

Operation

- The individual department: info
- Practical problems
- Behavioral leadership adjustments
- Concrete goal-setting

Answer the questions:
1. How is my department running?
2. Which challenges do we face right now?
3. How do we handle those challenges?
4. What do I need to return to?

FIGURE 11.3 Meeting forums where you can work with leadership of strategy and operation

and discuss the problems and challenges that face your company. As a rule, reciprocal brainstorming about the most appropriate leadership positions provides more clarity and workable certainty than working alone.

I often use a model to illustrate a shared leadership focus when I work with management groups who are in the process of developing their shared leadership approach. I have found the model to be useful when managers want to discuss leadership at a management group meeting. The model contains three meeting forums: a strategic meeting forum, a leadership meeting forum, and an operation-oriented meeting forum. The model is shown in Figure 11.3.

Most companies have a meeting structure that contains strategy meetings and operation meetings. They refer to them as management meetings. However, the question of how leadership can best create strategy, and how that connects to the operation, is often not considered in management groups. The questions about how we should lead in relation to relevant challenges (the arrow from strategy to leadership) are important to discuss so that we can collectively create meaning from complexity, and work towards workable certainty. This meeting forum in the management group is an important step toward reflective leadership.

The shared reflective distance should allow managers to find an optimal position in regard to concrete problems within their individual departments. In the following section, I will describe what it means to position yourself regarding leadership paradoxes. I will also present a tool which can help you use reflection to create balance between the alternatives within the paradoxes of leadership.

Positioning theory

Positioning theory, which was developed by Harré and Van Langenhove (1999), is essentially a critique of the idea that roles, norms, rules, and fixed guidelines determine how we act in a given situation. For example, according to role theory, you could determine a manager's strengths and weaknesses by using a test, feedback, and studies of how he acts. This would allow you to know something about his preferred role in the organization. In contrast, positions are something that are constantly produced through sense-making activities and the process of negotiating social life.

In this context, positioning means that a manager's behavior provides a voice to the alternatives in the leadership paradox. This is accomplished by knowing that positioning is acting out of only one part of a more complex problem.

Managers must ask themselves which leadership focus is needed in the organization and adjust leadership action accordingly. In contrast to integrative thinking, positioning is more of a leadership balancing act, where the scales are shifted according to need. Managers position themselves according to organizational needs, and they always use reflective distance to evaluate whether this position should change. This way of operating is called oscillation.

As we saw in the CVF model, this oscillation is determined by increasing or decreasing two contradictory leadership positions within the quadrants of change–stability or relationships–results. Oscillation means that a manager can only occupy one position at a time. Positioning allows the manager to occupy one role at a time while simultaneously relating to the other roles and switching when necessary. This allows the manager to turn to face alternatives in the paradox as well as turning his or her back on them – at the same time.

Oscillation requires reflection. It is important for managers and management groups to consider which leadership position is most relevant to any given organizational problem. In the book, *Paradoxical Thinking*, Fletcher & Olwyler (1997) describe a method that can easily be used by managers. This method is called Fletcher's pendulum, and allows oscillation to be supported by a particular way of relating to paradox.

The method allows managers to actively relate to both ends of the paradox – separately. An example of a leadership paradox could be: "We need to secure this order, and I know the best way to approach the sales meeting!" (= the manager goes first and shows the way) vs. "My employees in this sales department need to learn to take charge and feel ownership of the clients." (= the manager stays in the background and allows the employees to make decisions with a high degree of involvement).

The essential paradox in this example is trust–control. Should the manager lead the way and focus on the short-term goal of securing the client, which will create immediate results due to his own skills, *or* should the manager stay in the background and demonstrate trust that the employees can solve the task, and therefore risk that the order isn't secured? When dealing with a control–trust paradox, each solution can be logical. It is therefore best to ask when it is most beneficial to increase control and when it is most beneficial to cultivate trust and employee growth.

When working with a paradox, a manager can oscillate (take on different positions) depending on how the situation is evaluated. One way of working is to examine the advantages and disadvantages of a position and evaluate them based on what the organization is in the process of achieving.

We can use the trust–control paradox as an example. Let's imagine an example where there is a sales department that needs to achieve immediate results, but that also needs to develop the sales ability of the employees. The process toward workable certainty could resemble the one in Figure 11.4. It is important to stress that this is just an example constructed for the purpose of illustrating positioning. The pitfalls could be different, depending on the logic behind them. There could also be different connections that were relevant, and the employees' need for leadership should be taken into account, as well as the possible effects of each approach to leadership.

This approach to managerial reflection requires that managers try to remain neutral regarding their own preferences, and instead try to consider the advantages and disadvantages for the organization, the employees, and customer relations. In the above example, the manager must also determine which advantages there are in relation to the board of directors. It is not always necessary to consider so many perspectives as there are in this example, but the important thing is that relevant perspectives are considered so that the consequences for the organization can be evaluated. For some of these perspectives, it is necessary that the manager avoids acting without thinking, and therefore avoids creating opposition or a lack of understanding from the board, colleagues, or employees. Considering all of these perspectives allows the manager to map out a situation where he or she can create a logical leadership position (seen in relation to the concrete organizational problems and needs) rather than only being able to defend his or her position based on personal preferences. Therefore, the manager's choice becomes a reflective and active choice between contradictory alternatives.

The question can then be asked: don't we have a dilemma here? The answer is, yes: in the short term (the concrete situation), the manager has divided the poles in the paradox and acted by choosing to focus on one of the options. This is indeed characteristic of a dilemma – there is a choice where one alternative is chosen at the cost of another. However, the difference is that the manager has not made a

Position 1: Control
Do the task yourself and achieve results

Advantages:

- The manager is a role model and shows how things should be done.
- We ensure that the task succeeds. We ensure profit.
- We ensure that the customer receives the best consultant.
- The board of directors will see concrete order-intakes.

A solution when:

- The company is dependent on the current order.
- Employees are under training.
- The manager's professional skills need to be "illustrated."
- The employees have attempted to do the task and have reported that they can not – and the manager is in agreement.
- During "crisis-management."

Disadvantages:

- The manager is a role model and therefore shows that it is best when he does the tasks himself.
- The customer is used to expecting the manager to solve his probems.
- The board of directors can begin to pressure the manager to become a highly productive employee, rather than a leader.

FIGURE 11.4 Exploration of contradictory positions within the paradox

final choice. He or she is still considering both types of leadership, and will continually make decisions about which focus to choose as he or she works with the trust–control paradox.

It is important to have the paradox as a guideline for reflection in relation to concrete situations. For example, it might make sense to allow a seller to control an order, even though it would have been easier to do it yourself. In this case, the manager has to evaluate each case on an individual basis and constantly find the boundary between trust and control. He needs to occupy a leadership position where he "holds up the paradox" while simultaneously choosing a position within the paradox. He creates a challenge for the organization at the same time that he solves the challenge. This is done through realizing that you don't solve the paradox, you mentally move through it. You take a position in the "either-or" situation that is presented by the paradox, but actions will be different according to the situation or the relationship to the type of problem, the needs of the organization, the needs of the employees, etc.

Participants in my workshops about leadership often ask if oscillation is the same as situational leadership. You could indeed say that it is, just that it includes additional elements that aren't normally connected with the concept of situation-based leadership. In Hersey & Blanchard's (1996) model of situational leadership, the employees are the object of the manager's reflection and his or her decision regarding leadership action. In situational leadership, the manager organizes his or her leadership style based on an evaluation of two parameters: employee motivation and job maturity. Paradoxical leadership differs in that it explicitly asks the manager to use the company's goals and needs as the basis for choosing the approach to the employees. In paradoxical leadership, the leadership approach is not as clearly defined on a one-problem-one solution basis. For example, although a manager decides to take over in a sales situation, which could be the case in the above example, he or she maintains an awareness of the problems that those actions could cause for the organization. For example, he could step in and take responsibility for meeting with the client, but ensure that an employee is present and that they discuss the process after the meeting. This would potentially allow them to switch roles for the next client meeting. Another example could be that the employee holds the meeting, but that manager is present and observes, etc. The goal is not to clearly determine a leadership style, but to continually choose a focus, and be ready to address any problems that arise as a result of that choice.

Oscillation means that the manager takes stock of the situation and then creates meaning through an analysis of the short-term and long-term advantages and disadvantages of a particular form of action. Some questions to ask when working toward workable certainty could be:

- What are the alternative positions that I could occupy here?

For each of the alternatives:

- What advantages are there in this position in relation to what we want to accomplish in the organization? What are the disadvantages?
- What are the short-term advantages of the potential results? What are the short-term disadvantages?
- What advantages are there in this alternative in relation to the central interests of the company? What are the disadvantages?
- What are the advantages for the employees? What are the disadvantages?
- In which situations would this alternative clearly be the correct choice?
- In which situations would this alternative clearly create problems for the company?

If you can't find any disadvantages for the organization or its interests, then you are not working with a paradox. In addition, if the paradox is characterized by apparently contradictory sets of logic, and yet you can't solve the problem using this model and find that the problem only gets more complicated, it may be because the problem has a simple solution.

Relating to leadership as an area of dynamic and shifting organizational options allows you to pay attention to both your preferred and less desirable leadership positions. Unless you are aware of these elements of your behavior, you risk practicing unreflective leadership. This will result in you leading based on your preferred conclusions regarding what is most effective (easiest) for you, rather than what is most useful to your company or institution.

Summary

Paradoxical leadership needs to pay attention to the following points:
A double exploration of the positions within a paradox allows for:

- An acceptance of complexity in your leadership.
- A reflective distance – to *understand* and *relate to* the contradictory demands in concrete situations.
- You to be aware of your own preferred leadership style – *you will always turn your back on something.*
- You to consciously work to develop your leadership style repertoire – through awareness of your "right leg" and "left leg" in leadership positions – or through ensuring that "the left leg" will be taken on by someone else in the team.
- You to navigate flexibly – dependent on the situation and the needs of the organization.
- You to reflectively occupy a particular position in relation to your employees and your organization.
- You to use that position to talk with your employees and invite them into the discourse that is guiding your actions.

The management of positioning in paradoxes requires that managers consciously work with, and investigate, the leadership behavior and leadership tools that are most effective when working from a particular position.

> **REFLECTION: OSCILLATION**
>
> 1. Which positions are particular easy for me to occupy? Which leadership tools do I use in that position?
> 2. Which positions are unfamiliar to me? Which tools could be useful for me here? Are there colleagues, superiors, or former managers that could provide inspiration?
> 3. Which position does my organization/management team/employees/the situation need me to occupy right now so that we can succeed?

The leadership discipline requires that you are always able to use doubt – the doubt of how you lead in relation to the needs of the organization. Occupying a particular leadership position requires a flexible and investigative approach to your own leadership behavior. This allows you to continually adjust your actions through positioning. This demands what we could call organizational intelligence: the ability to read strategy, organization, core tasks, and the relevant challenges to employees in a given situation.

The solution to paradox is paradoxical: You must know yourself well enough to know your preferred leadership style. You will have a tendency to interpret information based on the leadership styles that make things easiest for you, due to a fear or insecurity that is connected to the other leadership styles. However, it is essential for your leadership and the needs of the organization that you are able to question you own preferences, read your organization's needs, and occupy the positions that match those current – and oscillating – needs.

12
ACCEPTANCE

As this book has highlighted, the basic approach to leadership is characterized as a complex phenomenon which cannot and should not be simplified. Simplifying problems and ignoring complexity does not solve organizational problems. Leadership needs to match complexity through practicing complex approaches. Complex approaches are necessary both for organizational complexity as well as for maintaining the role complexity and contradictory affiliations that are part of being in an organization.

Paradoxes illuminate inherent tension within an organization. Examples of this tension are the paradoxes of stability and change, well-being and efficiency, and centralization and decentralization. In this chapter, I will argue that acceptance is an important aspect of working in organizations, and can be accomplished through working with paradoxes. Acceptance should not be understood as resignation, but rather as a way of acting that arises when confronting complex and paradoxical problems. This allows for an understanding that complexity is a foundation for working with leadership, rather than a thing to be eliminated.

Acceptance in regard to working with paradoxes of belonging was one of the results of the sense-making dialogue meetings that were held during the Lego session. The managers had experienced feelings of paralysis, insecurity, and confusion during the large processes of change that were happening in the organization. There was a tendency to use scapegoats, accusations, and projections. These deflections were especially prominent in regard to senior management. The lack of clarity was perceived as a lack of clarity in senior management, and the owner and his CEO were blamed for causing confusing messages within the organization.

Working with the clear–ambiguous paradoxes that we found in the paradoxes of belonging (trust vs. control, autonomy vs. coordination, authenticity vs. loyalty, independence vs. dependence, etc.) allowed us to be able to address the emotional aspect of these paradoxes. Among other elements, we addressed the ambivalence regarding thinking about individual roles and common adjustments in the team.

The Lego managers were eventually able to see how they had let themselves be paralyzed by the paradoxes of belonging. Statements like: "We can't do anything before we figure out what we want," "We have to find out where we are actually going with this!" and "The one hand doesn't know what the other hand is doing!!" or "I have to communicate this loyally and be authentic – but I don't agree with the message!" were often used when the managers were frustrated about the insecurity that arose as a result of the new approaches in the process of organizational change.

Accusing the directors or senior management of lacking clarity was a defensive way for the middle managers and employees to remain in a "passive" and expectant position. In the change processes, employees would often sit and wait and hope that the managers would be shown a direction that was clear and reduced confusion and obscurity in both the management group and among the employees.

It is partially correct that a manager's job is to create clarity and transparency for employees during a process of change, but it can often end up in a "blaming game" between managers and employees. This can be attributed to organizational complexity.

Let's examine the vicious circle: It is normal that employees have difficulty orienting themselves regarding direction, meaning, and connection when the organization is undergoing change. The result is often paralysis and pronounced holding positions. When employees do not work with the changes, management will not be able to continually act in response to the problems that arise. This can lead to a situation where management might interpret the situation as if the employees are resistant to change.

The blaming game goes like this: Senior management can't communicate any more clearly, and feel that everything they can see is communicated clearly; meanwhile, the employees can't start implementing the changes before they have more knowledge about the meaning behind the changes and what is expected of them. Where does change start? This becomes a vicious circle: Management waits for employees to "get started," so that any confusion can become visible, while the employees wait for a "clear message" before they will commit to anything within the process of change.

Let's look at the following example: The vicious circle may become unbearable, which puts senior management under pressure to come out with a clear message. Therefore, they may choose to say, for example, "We need to close down our production in 6 months! We are going to merge with another big company." Senior management might think that they have removed any confusion by giving employees a clear message, but instead they will just create new problems. For example, "They just said that we needed to reduce our use of external partners, and now they want to close down production," or "They just said that we should be competitive in regard to production, but now they say that we have to outsource." The more that senior management feel they are communicating clearly, the bigger the chance that employees will notice the ambiguity and contradictions that can always be found within the messages. If requirements for full clarity and rationality are dominant in a company, it can mean the rise of a vicious circle, "blaming game," and simplification approach (an approach that attributes a lack of clarity to complexity somewhere in the organization). However, this doesn't solve anything. Full disclosure is not the answer.

Working toward workable certainty means that managers and employees must accept that paradoxes are a part of an organization undergoing change. Normally, we would say that the acceptance of something means that there is nothing we can do about it. However, in paradoxical thinking, acceptance means changing our understanding of the organization's problems. In other words, it means accepting ambiguity and complexity as the fundamental conditions for change. We could say that change comes before clarity, which is also a condition for change. Paradoxically, contradictory messages are often simultaneously true. Both employees and managers need to accept this fact. For example: clear messages lead to questions, innovation sparks the need for stability in working procedures, mergers energize tensions between merging and holding on to former corporate identity, etc.

The acceptance of paradoxes means that clarity must continually be co-created through interactions between managers and employees. There is a double dependency between the insight that employees achieve when solving tasks, and the opportunities for managers to create overview, guidelines, and advice, as well as appropriate support of the employees. Employees are dependent on clarity and messages from management, as well as support and involvement. Managers are dependent on using the insight and experience that employees have from solving their tasks. Without this insight, managers cannot properly organize their leadership approach. Therefore, acceptance also means that employees need to participate in a mutual sense-making session where they provide the manager with the opportunity to create the necessary overview. The connection and dependency work both ways as shown in Figure 12.1.

If we accept the premise that meaning and workable certainty must continually be co-created, we can see that managers are deeply dependent on the problems

FIGURE 12.1 Mutual sense-making, manager–employee relationship

that are brought in from various employees, teams, etc. in order to create workable certainty. All kinds of ambiguities can arise during the solution of problems. For example, if employees can't see how cost reduction harmonizes with the extra work that needs to be done, or if they get a message about supporting a department that should be closed, it is essential that the paradoxes, ambiguities, and dilemmas are brought to the manager's attention so that he or she can have the opportunity to create meaningful leadership practice. Therefore, managers can use the model from Figure 12.1 in order to communicate their expectations, feedback, and leadership positions to the employees. The employees also need to accept that clarity does not only come from senior management, but that it needs to continually be created through the interaction between the various levels of the organization.

Awareness of the paradoxical nature of organizations and change reduces the tendency to accuse senior management. This is accomplished through shifting focus toward helping managers and employees discover ways to live with the tensions created by paradoxes. When this happens, management is able to recognize paradoxes and contribute to development and change within the dynamic limitations of the organization. Here is an example:

> In a team where the employees were dissatisfied with their manager, it was revealed that some of the team members thought that it was important that the manager provided direction and told them what should happen and what was expected of the team as a whole. The logic behind this desire was that the manager should gather his team and help them to see how they utilized synergy and became a stronger team. Other team members thought that the manager should look at each individual employee's need for support, and do "casework" at the meetings. The logic behind this thought was that if they could work with the concrete tasks of each individual team member, they would be able to monitor each other and see what everyone was doing. They also thought that each employee had a need for clarity regarding concrete tasks.
>
> Therefore, the big question was if the team meetings should have a shared agenda when there was a shared theme that influenced the meeting, with the goal of creating a tight-knit team, *or* if concrete, more individual problems regarding tasks should have priority in the meetings so that the individual could get help and leave the meeting knowing how to proceed.
>
> During the discussion, the team members noticed that the shared-theme logic and the individuality logic could be understood in connection to one another: In order to be a homogeneous team, it was necessary to focus on differences and the individual situations. At this point, the polarities of the paradox were accepted, and the team members and manager agreed that they should give the manager enough information about their individual problems so that he could bring them up at the meetings, and discuss how each problem could be relevant for the other team members, and how they should all be involved in the solution of the problem. If, however, the manager

determined that there was a problem that should be considered for a joint discussion, individual examples would be used to support the discussion.

Managers need their employees to work with them and be willing to follow them into the realm of insecurity. Ralph Stacey (2000), who works with complexity theory, states that organizational change is about being able to act with intention when heading into the unknown. The unknown is a part of change. However, I see many companies with employees who demand clarity before they can (or will) act. Acceptance means accepting that the unknown cannot be communicated in a way that makes it "known."

For example, senior management in a production company will encounter a paradox when they discuss whether they should spend more time constructing and describing the process for launching new products. This paradox calls for stable procedures in order for the company to be efficient within the pressurized environment of the market, but will simultaneously result in managers feeling that all the documentation and focus on the procedures is a waste of time, and interferes with the pace of production. In other words, the paradox lies in the fact that speed is often best achieved through thorough attention to detail. The paradox is a "built in" part of the problem.

In my experience, managers and employees who accept the terms of the paradox begin to be able to see the "ambiguous" signals from senior management as a reflection of a broader organizational challenge. When this happens, they feel that they can do something about the problem. In other words, when the managers accept that paradoxes are a fundamental part of their organization, they are able to find the motivation to work with the organizational ambiguity created by complexity and paradoxes. However, this requires that managers ensure that everyone in the organization is able to find workable certainty, and realize that although employees crave certainty, the creation of full certainty is impossible. All organizational members must agree to operate in accordance with a fixed plan *and* accept that plans change constantly due to new "certainties."

Acceptance: a paradoxical solution

Paradoxes are especially problematic for organizations that operate out of formal logic (thinking in dichotomies such as "either-or," "true-false," "effective-ineffective," etc.). When considered in terms of formal logic, paradoxes are often perceived as contradictions, as well as a source of frustration, ambiguity, or paralysis. This results in one alternative being chosen at the cost of another. For example, in projects regarding organizational change, we often see that the old form of the organization is "replaced" by new methods.

This tendency to "replace" the old can lead to the idea that the new approaches (e.g. a new approach to marketing, management, sales, or strategy) will solve the problems that were created by old ways of thinking. In other words, formal logic leads to the belief that it is most efficient to completely transform the way of thinking within an organization. However, the tension created by paradoxes (e.g. centralization–decentralization, downsizing–development, management–independence, differentiation–integration) is not removed by choosing one of the options. Accepting paradoxes as a condition of organizational life is the only way to include both alternatives of the paradox.

For example, if a large organization with many departments chooses to decentralize the budget, it becomes difficult to think of the organization as a whole, and the individual departments risk sub-optimizing in order to promote their individual results. However, if the organization chooses to centralize the budget, it risks producing a lack of responsibility and competitive spirit because the individual departments are unable to see where their tasks have been successful. Therefore, many companies choose to find solutions that balance the centralizing–decentralizing paradox. However, the problem has not disappeared. It continues to exist within organizational life in the form of a paradox. Other examples of this type of paradox are individual rewards versus collective goals and differentiation in work methods versus a shared company profile.

Organizations need to work with a general acceptance that organizational life is inherently paradoxical. Managers must address these paradoxes – together with subordinates – in order to embrace paradoxical thinking, instead of vicious circles or splitting between top and bottom of the organization (although I accept that sometimes there may be other reasons for such a split).

Acceptance consists of the paradoxical fact that paradoxes must be managed, not solved. This requires the acknowledgement that paradoxes are made up of apparent contradictions, which we must consider in order to act. However, this does not mean that paradoxes can (or should) be solved. Instead, it means that paradoxes are a way of relating to the inherent complexity of organizations.

Creating acceptance within the organization

Accepting organizational paradoxes is easier said than done. However, acceptance is necessary in order to solve complex problems. It can be tempting for managers to communicate one-dimensionally when employees ask for clarity, simplicity, transparency, etc. Therefore, if a manager has discovered a paradox, it is essential that he or she shares it with the organization. How can he or she do this? In my work as a consultant, I have seen many managers succeed in creating workable certainty for employees who are working in a complex reality. Here is a list of the things that a manager will need to accomplish:

- **Create continual clarity** regarding the overall direction. Where are we going, and what will management prioritize in the near future (not once and for all – but continually)?
- **Explain the logic of your decisions**: We have chosen to increase the demands placed on you (results) … because … and yet we want to manage the team's well-being and high stress level (relationships) by …

- **Share complex problems** with the employees (e.g. that you are in the process of determining the placement of the administration in connection with the current organizational change). Tell them about the considerations that you have to make and listen to their comments. Take their feedback into consideration.
- **Present both ends of the paradox**, for example: We need to find ways to introduce the new team structure – and we need to do it in such a way that individual performance can still be recognized. Or: our strategy is to increase growth by X percent, but we need to find new ways to focus and maintain cooperation in the middle of these challenges.
- **Be present/available**: Be available for conversations with employees and be ready to answer questions such as "How does this connect with …?" and "What does this mean for me".

The point about availability is important, both to be able to approach employees (a clear managerial advantage), and to help employees manage the paradox and accept the ambiguities, complex problems, and contradictory demands that are part of the process of change. Employees need to be supported in order to work within the situation and create workable certainty for themselves. Availability, and being there to converse with employees, is essential in combating the resistance which is often found within organizational change. Resistance can be seen as a polarization, where employees responsibly point out the part of the paradox to which the manager has apparently turned his or her back. It is important that the manager listens to the employees and thinks about how he or she can relate to their points. There might not always be a clear way to respond, but it is important to investigate the problem in collaboration with the employees, because they might have a solution. Availability also means helping employees create enough meaning to be able to act (create workable certainty).

Summary

Effective leadership is closely related to the ability to accept complexity and paradoxes as a basis for management. In order to be decisive and act with purpose, managers must accept paradoxes as an inherent part of organizational change. Acceptance should be understood as an active way of making sense out of complexity, and helping the organization (colleagues, management, and employees) make sense and move toward more workable certainty.

In 1945, Scott Fitzgerald described high intelligence as the ability to work with two contradictory ideas and still maintain the ability to function. In the same way, intelligent leadership is the ability to communicate in a way that includes contradictory ideas and demonstrates goal-driven behavior, while simultaneously maintaining integrity, trustworthiness, and direction. Effective managers have the ability to be in complex, contradictory, and paradoxical situations, and act decisively in complex, contradictory, and paradoxical problems, while still providing meaning, direction, and clarity for the employees.

> **REFLECTION: ACCEPTANCE**
>
> 1. How do you typically tackle ambiguity in strategy?
> 2. How do you share these ambiguities within the management team?
> 3. To what degree do you attempt to remove the paradox (i.e. to create clear answers to problems)?
> 4. Acting with intention regarding uncertainty – what does that mean to you?

We have now seen how the acceptance of complexity can help managers work within paradoxes, instead of "eliminating" them. Being able to collectively reflect on and make sense from the contradictions involved in processes of change will reduce frustration and create collective curiosity. This requires a willingness to use integrative thinking, create reflective distance in order to position yourself regarding leadership positions, and create acceptance of the fact that paradoxes are here to stay. Paradoxes want something from us … they want to be framed, managed, and accepted in creative and complex solutions.

13
MANAGERIAL FLOW
Leading through paradox

In the last 15–20 years, Danish business managers have been offered numerous tool-oriented courses. How can you help your employees "own" the company vision? How do you involve them? What does autonomy look like in practice, and how do you strengthen employee autonomy? How do you create good, trustworthy teamwork, and how do you coach the employees to find their own way and have better ownership for the solutions? How do you create a strategy for the company, and how do you share that strategy so that everyone follows it? Managers and consultants have worked with all of these "how" questions over the years. The questions are good and practical, and the answers are provided in the form of learning new approaches and techniques from courses, leadership books, trainings, etc.

At first glance, paradoxical leadership is not a leadership technology. Rather it provides a framework for matching organizational complexity. Paradox is a way of thinking. Leadership should be understood as working to reduce organizational complexity to the degree that members find workable certainty. Sense-making processes through reflective leadership are the fulcrum of paradoxical leadership.

Paradoxical leadership also means that the leadership task moves between various paradigms and discourses. It means that you need to take three steps: The first is the recognition of the paradox. The second is being able to see the strengths and weaknesses in each alternative. The third, and most challenging, is to avoid the pitfall of choosing one alternative and thinking in terms of "either-or" solutions. Using paradoxes as a starting point, you will be able to see "both-and" solutions. You will be able to see the connection between alternatives. At this point you will be able to react to paradoxes using paradoxical thinking. This means that you will be able to see both alternatives, include both, and still act based on one of them. You need to have a complex response to a complex phenomenon. In this book, you have read about paradoxes in three levels: organizational paradoxes, role paradoxes, and paradoxes of belonging. The category of the paradox is not as important to your leadership practice as the ability to work with them through integrative thinking, reflective distance, and positioning. It is also important that your company is able to accept that the world is complex, and is able to avoid being caught in rational "either-or" thinking and one-sided decision-making. The acceptance of complexity as a fundamental aspect of organizations (and especially organizations undergoing change) is a condition for allowing the members of the organization to operate within paradoxes.

Paradoxes are interwoven

Paradoxes become even more visible when we examine how they are connected. Organizational paradoxes, role paradoxes, and paradoxes of belonging are inseparably connected. For example, when the Lego managers and I discussed how their roles in the organization (in the form of role paradoxes) contained ambiguities, they were able to discuss both the insecurity resulting from senior management's messages (the organizational paradox) and how these ambiguities affected their relationships to one another (the paradox of belonging). The ambiguous messages about expectations of leadership roles resulted in managers not wanting to share resources, since they did not feel safe regarding what constituted success. ("What if they can't see my performance?) The paradoxes of belonging were strengthened by the ambiguity and insecurity of the role paradoxes.

This connection means that what can be understood as a role paradox on one level can also be reflected as a paradox of belonging and/or an organizational paradox.

> In the Lego project, many managers were in doubt about whether they should concentrate on ensuring efficiency in production (and creating stability) or changing the production line and employee work processes in

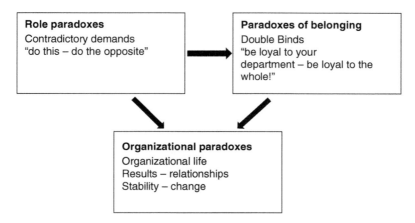

FIGURE 13.1 The connection between paradoxes

order to launch new forms of production. The employees (including unions, etc.) thought that the organization shouldn't institute more change right now, while management wanted to increase demands on performance and new forms of production in order to create stability. The role paradox of supporting–challenging (one of the role paradoxes in CVF) was clear: The employees needed to be supported – and at the same time, senior management demanded that they be challenged.

The managers agreed that the employees were overwhelmed, and wanted to postpone the project regarding new forms of production. However, at the same time, they knew that they would end up disappointing someone, no matter what they did. In addition, it was difficult to discuss this double affiliation (the paradox of belonging between representing management and maintaining employee motivation and trust) as well as the paralysis that resulted from the need to succeed in both halves of the paradox.

The anxiety level was high. The managers were dependent on the employees in order to succeed, and management did not see any problem in the tension that the managers experienced between trying to accommodate the needs of both the employees and management.

When the manager group consulted senior management with this difficult dilemma, the answer was simply that there was no contradiction, and that the organization needed to succeed in achieving stability as well as change (organizational paradox). Senior management's attitude was, "You need to figure it out! And you need to succeed despite the insecurity that is connected to what it means to succeed!" It became the managers' role to balance within the role paradox, confront and manage their own ambivalence regarding ambiguous demands, and find acceptance and action within the framework of the organizational paradox between stability and change.

This example shows how paradoxes are connected. It can be difficult to see which type of paradox you are experiencing in a given situation. However, it is not as important to identify the type of paradox as it is to know that they exist and show themselves in the following ways:

1. As contradictory tensions in the organizational life (e.g. results–relations/change–stability).
2. As ambiguity regarding which roles (positions) are necessary to occupy in order to succeed in leading the organization in a chosen direction (e.g. supportive–challenging/visionary–practical).
3. As ambivalence, contradictory feelings, and attachment to the organization (e.g. trust–control/team work–individualism).

Therefore, leadership is about creating workable certainty by reducing the complexity just enough to allow it to be understood, and therefore allow for intentional action. To help with this process, I have introduced the Competing Values Framework (CFV) as a model to simplify complexity while offering a model for reflection. This reflection allows for the creation of a shared language that can be used to discuss the contradictory challenges of an organization.

Using the CVF model can also help manager groups to discuss which leadership role paradoxes need attention, as well as how they can collaboratively address and evaluate their leadership practice. Leadership is often a broad concept. How can you measure your own leadership performance? How can you determine which other positions might be useful? The Competing Values Framework provides a model for working with your leadership development.

Paradoxes: a leadership mindset

Paradoxical leadership is both concrete and abstract. Paradoxes are a difficult phenomenon to grasp, which is perhaps why they are the subject of so many philosophy books. At their worst, paradoxes are a source of frustration, confusion, and paralysis. However, at their best, they are a "brainteaser" and a way to challenge managers to reflect on the complexity of organizational problems. This reflection is necessary, as long as the manager does not attempt to remove the contradictory demands, interests, understandings, tasks, and feelings that are an inherent part of daily leadership challenges. Leadership means acting with intent when facing the ambiguous, the complex, and the undecidable. It means acting with intention as well as being open to the complexities that cannot be solved.

Managing the paradoxes of leadership requires active reflection. The following points describe three ways to achieve this reflection:

1. **Integrative thinking**, where managers attempt to solve problems by considering both alternatives at the same time.
2. **Positioning**, which occurs through reflective distance in determining which position you should occupy between two polarities. This approach supports a decision about how to act. Since you cannot act within a paradox, you have to turn your back on one alternative for now – but you need to choose a position based on the strategic, human, and visionary focus of the organization.
3. **Acceptance** of paradoxes as fundamental elements of your organizations. This is a fundamental assumption if you want to lead within complexity instead of attempting to simplify. The acceptance of paradoxes as a fundamental aspect of organizational reality means that you always need to reflect on the paradoxes and unsolvable situations, but realize that you still have to make a decision.

Paradoxes require you to continually challenge your leadership position. In the box below, you will find some of the questions that you need to continually ask yourself in order to recognize that paradoxes are an integral part of your leadership practice.

> ## REFLECTIONS: LEADERSHIP THROUGH PARADOX
>
> ### Organizational paradoxes:
>
> 1. Which contradictions am I experiencing in connection with the changes and demands of the organization at the moment?
> 2. How do we maintain balance between (e.g.) stability and change?
> 3. How do we maintain balance between (e.g.) quick results and ensuring that employees work well together?
>
> ### Role paradoxes:
>
> 1. Which paradoxical demands are we experiencing right now? Which paradoxical tasks?
> 2. How can we decide to balance/act within these paradoxes?
> 3. What kind of a plan should we propose to the director/board in order to succeed?
> 4. What will this require of each manager? Will the demands be different for various departments/managers?
>
> ### Paradoxes of belonging:
>
> Discuss these paradoxes in your manager group, even though it takes courage:
>
> 1. What is going on between us as a manager group? What is going on between me and my employees?
> 2. What feelings are involved (fear of failure, loneliness, paralysis, giving up, doubt, anger, etc.)?
> 3. How can we best manage these feelings in order to maintain our momentum?
> 4. How can we support one another?

In the article, "Release the paradoxes!" ("Slip paradokserne løs!") (2008), Klaus Majgaard writes that paradoxes come alive when we accept them as fundamental aspects of organizations, and realize that they don't need to be solved or balanced. Paradoxes are accepted once we constantly create and maintain organizations as elements of a pattern of interaction:

> We choose to remain in the tension of the paradox – we can at least reformulate the sides in the paradox and thereby create new meaning and reveal new opportunities for action. "Paradox, of course, cannot be resolved or harmonized, only endlessly transformed" (Stacy, 2007, p. 441).
>
> *Majgaard (2011, p. 20)*

Majgaard suggests role-play and situational play as ways to work with organizational paradoxes. Play allows managers to meet paradoxes, accept them, reinterpret them, and brainstorm options. It is clear that our habitual decision-making strategies (when we choose one alternative) are difficult to overcome. However, having paradoxes as a tool in the leadership toolbox allows you to create a reflective leadership practice. This should allow you to include the complexity and contradictory solutions that are inherent in paradoxes.

Leadership concepts of the future: do they include paradoxes?

Sometimes you tend to find what you are looking for. It can be hard to determine if I see paradoxes everywhere because I work with them, and they make sense everywhere I encounter them, or if I see paradoxes (in leadership literature, companies, lectures, managers' desire for a concept which they can understand and relate to) because there is currently increased focus on leadership that includes complexity. Regardless of which option is true, it appears that the paradoxical perspective is becoming more and more common as a way of managing organizational ambiguity.

The book *Contradictions in Organization and Leadership Theory* (*Modstillnger I organisations- og ledelseteori*) (Høpner et al., 2010) argues that a theoretical and paradigmatic juxtaposition would help the reader to think in and operate according to juxtapositions, in order to understand complex realities. The book examines the double-edged tendencies that are found within various organizational phenomena: strategies where theorists argue for planning, contrasted with more fluctuating theories about strategy as a continuous process.

Goleman, Stacey, Luhmann, Adize, Hersey & Blanchard, Drucker, Høpner et al., and many other leadership theorists argue for balanced leadership. There are many definitions of leadership, but the paradoxical definition is that everything has something to offer. Paradoxical leadership goes between the paradigms that these theories are built on, and advocates an approach where leadership is about both integrating the approaches in a transcendent new way, and about knowing that you have to choose when one or the other approach needs to be dominant in your leadership practice.

The companies that are used as examples in this book are mostly private companies (businesses, production companies, or similar). Most of the companies I work with experience challenges in placing leadership on the agenda. It is seen as a complex issue, and few managers want to have leadership and organization as their primary interest and focus. Paradoxical leadership offers a theoretical framework that can be used to understand the leadership task in all of its complexity. For example, I have participated in some turnaround processes where the strategic focus needs to be changed, and where the Competing Values Framework has been useful in working with changes within the company. It allows the manager group to have a shared language and a shared focus on complex and ambiguous challenges. This helps the manager group to be able to organize the task together, and to collectively move the company in the right direction.

Businesses all have a shared characteristic: they often face the same organizational paradoxes as a fundamental aspect of their business. These paradoxes include:

- Red Ocean strategy versus Blue Ocean strategy
- Creativity in production versus prompt delivery
- Thinking best versus thinking cheapest
- Niche-production versus mass-production
- People versus results

There are many business paradoxes, but the public sector experiences the same amount of paralytic pressure.

I have not used so many examples of public institutions in this book. This is not because paradoxes do not exist in the public sector, but simply because more of my work has been in the private sector. However, my work with public institutions has also provided countless examples of how a paradoxical perspective can be useful. Here are a few examples:

The Danish education system is now working with the concept of inclusion in the classroom. Among other things, this means that schools must not exclude the children who have difficulties sitting still or understanding the teacher, but must include these children in the classroom. Here are some of the potential paradoxes: The teacher as a manager versus as a pedagogue (inclusion sometimes means setting boundaries that might not fit a child), PPRs' (school psychologists) role as experts versus consultants, etc.

Another example is the streamlining of daycare in Denmark: This requires that daycares cut costs while still maintaining a high level of professionalism. They need to work with the well-functioning children and focus on the socially vulnerable children. They need to centralize and decentralize their finances, etc.

Majgaard describes the many aspects of pressure that are placed on public institutions. For example, there is pressure regarding:

- Political competition and profiling demands versus the desire for continuity and long-term goals.
- Tight budgets versus ambitions for high quality and core values.
- Safe and effective operation versus the desire for innovation.
- Short-term performance demands versus long-term development goals.
- Approachability for demanding users versus the institutional integrity.
- Legal rights and standardization versus the need to develop unique relationships to citizens.
- The desire for central administration and organization versus the desire for decentralized autonomy and multiplicity (Majgaard, 2011).

Majgaard points out that:

> The emotional tones can vary when we are talking about pressure. It can lead to frustration and despair (the crushed public manager). Or it can radiate

obstinate decisiveness (the heroic public manager who can stand up to the pressure). Finally, it can also be clinical and bring a distanced and observant point of view – such as a systems theoretical analysis that draws attention to complexity, contingency, and paradox as fundamental conditions, without really having more at play.

The pressure is loaded with tension, anxiety, and potential anxiety under all of these circumstances. It reveals a situation where it's not about choosing resources for a given goal. The goal is in the competition and boundaries of the rational choices at stake. It can be small-scale in everyday choices. Or it can be a dramatic crisis.

Majgaard (2011, p. 6)

Over the last few years, I have found that many managers struggle with determining which position they should occupy within these fields. The more management is decentralized, the more pronounced the paradoxes. Paradoxes are useful when finding acceptance and maintaining decisiveness under pressure without escaping the pressure. Paradoxical thinking allows for finding a reflective way of matching the pressurized situations with the problems that arise, without choosing a side.

Conclusion

Paradoxes are confusing and ambiguous. Handy (1994, p. 47) writes: "To live with simultaneous opposites is, at first glance, a recipe for indecision at best, schizophrenia at worst." However, this doesn't have to be the case. Paradoxes can be found in many areas of life. Here are some examples: Should parents be both directive and understanding regarding their children? Organizations are structured and fluctuating, concerned with long-term perspectives in some areas but passionate about the here-and now in other areas. Managers, and other members of the organization, need to be able to create meaning in paradoxes, since paradoxes are increasingly a part of daily life. I would like to highlight Handy's point that the key to living with paradoxes is understanding them. Balancing and integrating paradoxes must not be random. A lack of understanding of the multifaceted truth and the inherent opportunities of paradoxes will result in ambiguous, paralyzing, and confusing communication. Leading with and through paradoxes is necessary in order to help the members of the organization create social meaning in their shared reality.

Examples from the Lego project and other companies have shown us various ways with which to meet paradoxes: First, through accepting that good leadership isn't found in "either-or" thinking, but that paradoxes are embedded in all organizational life. Second, through a continual evaluation of what you should act on within the paradox and what you should turn your back on. Third, the shared confrontation of your own double incentives, emotional attachments, and ambivalences.

If you apply a paradoxical perspective to a problem-solving culture, it can feel like being on a seesaw. You need to work together in order to create balance. If you view organizational problems through a paradoxical perspective, and the other person does as well, the seesaw ride can be fun and interesting. However, if the person sitting on the other end does not share, or obstructs, your attempt to include contradictory poles, the ride will fail. In other words, the sense-making processes are social and need to occur in collaboration with others. Although you might accept paradoxes and attempt to work with them, others can experience your efforts as inconsistent, ambiguous, unconnected, and without direction. On the other hand, if you do not grasp paradoxes and insist on seeing things from an "either-or" perspective, you risk rigidity and being unable to productively contribute to change. There is no way around it! The paradoxes of leadership provide the opportunity to increase awareness about apparently contradictory and ambiguous aspects of organizational life.

However, how can managers find flow in their leadership activities through paradoxes? They need to decide and act; create order from complexity and decide what is best for the organization.

Although I have suggested various tools with which to grasp and work with paradoxes, it is still an ambiguous solution. In other words, the solution to relating to paradoxes is, in itself, paradoxical, and it leads us to the following conclusion:

**Paradox is a mental construction and
can therefore be mentally dissolved
And
Paradox is inherent in all social life and
can therefore not be dissolved
– just lived!**

BIBLIOGRAPHY

Ackhoff, R.L.: Beyond Prediction and Preparation. *Journal of Management Studies*, vol. 20, no. 1, 1983.
Agervold, M., Jeppensen, H.J.: Uddelegering af ansvar og kompetence i et arbejdsmiljøperspektiv. I: *Arbejdspsykologisk Bulletin,* vol. 9, 1996, pp. 11–64.
Alvesson, M., Sveningsson, S.: Good visions, bad Micromanagement and ugly visions. Contradictions in (non-) leadership in a knowledge intensive organization. *Organization Studies*, vol. 24, no. 6, 2003, 961–988.
Andersen, N.Å., Born, A.W.: *Kaerlighed og omstilling – Italesaettelsen af den offentligt ansatte.* Nyt fra Samfundsvidenskaberne, København, 2001.
Andersen, T.: *Refleksive processer.* Dansk Psykologisk Forlag, København, 1996.
Argyris, C.: *On Organizational Learning.* Blackwell, Cambridge, 1995.
Bartunek, J.: The dynamics of personal and organizational reframing. In Quinn, R., Cameron, K.: *Paradox and Transformation: Toward a Theory of Change in Organization and Management.* Ballinger Publishing Company, Cambridge MA, 1988.
Berger, P.L., Luckmann, T.: *The Social Construction of Reality.* Doubleday, New York, 1966.
Bohm, D.: *On Dialogue.* Routledge, New York, 1996.
Burr, V.: *Social Constructionism*, Routledge, Sussex, 2003.
Cameron, K, Quinn, R.: *Diagnosing and Changing Organizational Culture: Based on the Competing Values Framework.* Jossey-Bass Business & Management Series, 2005.
Collins, J.C.: *Good to Great.* Harper Business, New York, 2001.
Csikzentmihaley, M: *Finding Flow: The Psychology of Engagement with Everyday Life.* Basic Books, New York, 1997.
Darmer, P.: The Subject(ivity) of Management. *Journal of Organizational Change Management,* vol. 13, 2000, pp. 334–351.
Denison, D.R, og Hooijberg, R., Quinn, R.E.: Paradox and performance: Toward a theory of behavioral complexity in managerial leadership. *Organization Science,* vol. 6, no. 5, 1995, pp. 524–540.
Dewey, J.: *How We Think.* Heath, New York, 1933.
Drucker, P.F.: *Management Tasks, Responsibilities, Practices.* Butterworth Heinemann, Oxford, 1999.

Dyer, J., Gregersen, H., Christensen, C.M.: *The Innovator's DNA*. Harvard Business Review Press, Boston, MA, 2011.
Farson, R.: *Management of the Absurd*. Simon & Schuster, New York, 1996.
Fletcher, G., Olwyler, J.: *Paradoxical Thinking*. Berrett-Koehler, San Francisco, 1997.
Ford, J.D., Backoff, R.W.: Organizational change in and out of Dualities and Paradox. In: Quinn, R.E, Cameron, K.S. (Eds.) *Paradox and Transformation: Toward a theory of Change in Organization and Management*. Ballinger Publishing Company, Cambridge, MA, 1988.
Ford, J.D., Ford, L.W.: Logics of identity, contradiction, and attraction in change. *Academy of Management Review*, vol. 19, 1994, pp. 756–795.
Frankl, V.: Paradoxical Intention and Dereflection. *Psychotherapy: Theory, Research, Practice.* Vol. 12, 1975, pp. 226–237.
Geertz, C.: *The Interpretation of Cultures*. Basic Books, New York, 1973.
Geertz, C.: *Local Knowledge: Further Essays in Interpretive Anthropology*. Basic Books, New York, 1983.
Gergen, K.J.: Social Psychology as Social Construction: The Emerging Vision. In *The Message of Social Psychology: Perspectives on Mind in Society*. McGarty, C. & Haslam, A. (Eds.). Blackwell, Oxford, 1997.
Gioia, D.A., Pitre, E.: Multiparadigm Perspectives on Theory Building. *Academy of Management Review*, vol.15, 1990, pp. 584–602.
Goleman, D.: Leadership that Gets Results. *Harvard Business Review*, March/April, 2000.
Goleman, D.: *Social Intelligence*. Random House, New York, 2006.
Hamel, G.: *The Future of Management*. Harvard Business School Press, New York, 2007.
Handy, C.: *The Age of Paradox*. Harvard Business School Press, New York, 1994.
Harré, R., van Langenhove, L.V: Introducing Positioning Theory. In Van Langenhove, L.V. & Harré, R. (Eds.). *Positioning Theory: Moral Contexts of Intentional Action*. Basil Blackwell Publishers, Oxford, 1999.
Hatch, M.J., Ehrlich, S.B.: Irony and the Social Construction of Contradiction in the Humor of a Management Team. *Organization Studies*, vol. 14, 1993, pp. 505–526.
Hennestad, B.W.: The Symbolic Impact of Double Bind Leadership. Double Bind and The Dynamics of Organizational Culture. *Journal of Management Studies*, vol. 3, 1990, pp. 265–280.
Hersey, P., Blanchard, K.H. *Management of Organizational Behavior: Utilizing Human Resources.* (7th edition) Prentice Hall, Upper Saddle River, NJ, 1996.
Høpner, J., Bendixen Sørensen, H., Jørgensen, T.B., Andersen, T., Senderovitz, M.: *Contradictions in Organization and Leadership Theory (Modstillinger i organisations- og ledelsesteori)*. Gyldendal Akademisk, Kbh, 2010.
Huxham, C., Vangen, S.: Ambiguity, Complexity and Dynamics in the Membership of Collaboration. *Human Relations*, vol. 53, 2000, pp. 771–806.
Isaacs, W.: *Dialogue and the Art of Thinking Together. A Pioneering Approach to Communicating in Business and in Life*. Doubleday, New York, 1999.
James, W.: *Pragmatism and the Meaning of Truth*. Harvard University Press, Cambridge, 1975.
Jensen, A.F.: *Mellem Ting. Foucaults filosofi*. Det Lille Forlag, Frederiksberg, 2005.
Kets de Vries, M.: *Organizational Paradoxes. Clinical Approaches to Management*. Routledge, London, 1995.
Kneer, G., Nassehi, A.: *Niklas Luhmann – introduktion til teorien om sociale systemer.* Hans Reitzels Forlag, København, 1997.
Kirkeby, O.F. *Organisationsfilosofi*. Samfundslitteratur, Frederiksberg, 2001.
Knudstorp, J.V.: Lego must learn the art of the impossible (in Danish: Lego skal laere det umuliges kunst). *Boersen*, September 9, 2005.

Lewis, M.W., Grimes, A.J.: Metatriangulation: Building Theory from Multiple Paradigms. *Academy of Management Review*, 1999, vol. 24, pp. 672–690.
Lewis, M.W.: Exploring Paradox; Toward a More Comprehensive Guide. *Academy of Management Review* 1999, vol. 24, pp. 672–690.
Lewis, M.W., Dehler, G.E.: Learning through paradox: A pedagogical strategy for exploring contradictions and complexity. *Journal of Management Education*, 2000, vol. 24, 708–725.
Lucas, J.R.: *Broaden the Vision and Narrow the Focus*. Greenwood Publishing Group, Westport, CT, 2006.
Luhmann, N.: *Iagttagelse og Paradox*. Gyldendal, København, 1998.
Lüscher, L.S.: *Working Through Paradox. An Action Research on Sensemaking at the Lego Company*, VDM –verlag, München, 2012.
Lüscher, L.S., Staerk, A.: Ledelse I det postmoderne – hvordan gør man det? (Leadership in the post-modern perspective: is it possible?) *Erhvervspsykologisk Tidsskrift, Psykologisk Forlag*, no 3, 2008.
Madsen, B.: Rod og Oprydning i Organisationen. In Kristensen, H. & Cawasje, S. (Eds.). *Bidrag fra Augustkonferencen 1996*, pp. 137–151, Psykologisk Institut, Aarhus, 1998.
Majgaard, C.: Slip Paradokserne løs! *Økonomistyring & Informatik*, nr. 3 2011.
March, J., Olsen, J.P.: *Ambiguity and Choice in Organisations*. University Press, 1976.
Martin, R.: *The Opposable Mind*. Harvard Business School of Publishing, Boston, MA, 2007.
Mead, G.H.: *Mind, Self and Society*. Chicago University Press, Chicago, 1934.
Northhouse, P.G.: *Leadership Theory and Practice*. Sage Publications, Thousand Oaks, CA, 1997.
Oelgaard, B.: *Kommunikation og Oekomentale systemer*. Akademisk forlag, Kbh, 2004.
Pearce, B.W.: *Interpersonal Communication. Making Social Worlds*. Harper Collins, New York, 1994.
Politiken Business Erhvervssider, October 28, 2009.
Poole, M.S., Van de Ven, A.: Using Paradox to Build Management and Organization Theories. *Academy of Management Review*, 1989, vol. 14, pp.562–578.
Putnam, L.: Contradictions and Paradoxes in Organizations. In: Thayer, L. (Ed.) *Organization Communications; Emerging Perspectives*, pp.151–167. Blex Publishing, Norwood, 1986.
Quinn, R.E., Cameron, K.S.: *Paradox and Transformation. Toward a Theory of Change in Organization and Management*. Ballinger Publishing Company, Cambridge MA, 1988a.
Quinn, R.E., Cameron, K.S.: *Beyond Rational Management. Mastering the Paradoxes and Competing Demands of High Performance*. Jossey-Bass Publishers, San Francisco, 1988b.
Rapoport, A.: Escape from Paradox. *Scientific American* vol. 217, 1967, pp. 50–56.
Sainsbury, R.M.: *Paradoxes*. 2nd edition. Cambridge University Press, Cambridge, 1995.
Sjöstrand, S.E.: *The Two Faces of Management. The Janus Factor*. International Thomson Business Press, London, 1997.
Slaatte, H.A.: *The Pertinence of the Paradox*. Humanities Press, New York, 1968.
Shotter, J.: *Conversational Realities: Constructing Life Through Language*. Sage Publications, London, 1993.
Smith, K., Berg, D.N.: *Paradoxes of Group Life*. Jossey-Bass Publishers, San Francisco, 1987.
Smith, K., Berg, D.N.: Paradox and Groups. In: Gillette, J. & McCollom, M. (Eds). *Groups in Context: A New Perspective on Group Dynamics*. Addison-Wesley, Reading, MA, 1990.
Soeholm, T.M., Storch, J., Juhl, A., Dahl, K., Molly, A.: *Ledelsesbaseret Coaching*. Boersen, København, 2006.
Stacey, R.: *Complexity and Management*, Routledge, London, 2000.
Stelter, R. (ed.): *Coaching: læring og udvikling*. Dansk Psykologisk Forlag, København, 2002.
Teunissen, J.: Paradoxes in Social Science and Research. In: Koot, W., Sabelis, I., Ybema, S. (Eds). *Contradictions in Context: Puzzling over Paradoxes in Contemporary Organizations*. VU University Press, Amsterdam, 1996.

Thygesen-Poulsen, P.: *Lego – en virksomhed og dens sjael*. Schultz, Albertslund, 1993.
Tomm, K.: Interventive Interviewing: Part II. Reflexive Questioning as a Means to Enable Self-Healing. *Family Process*, vol. 26, 1987, pp. 167–183.
Vince, R., Broussine, M.: Paradox, Defence and Attachment: Accessing and Working With Emotions an Relations Underlying Organizational Change. *Organizational Studies*, vol. 17, 1996.
Weick, K.E., Westley, F.: Organizational Learning. Affirming an Oxymoron (1996). In Clegg, S., Hardy, C., Nord, W.R.: *Managing Organizations: Current Issues*. Sage Books, 1999.
Weick, K.E.: *The Social Psychology of Organizing*. Addison-Wesley Publishing Co. Menlo Park, CA, 1969.
Weick, K.E: *Sensemaking in Organizations*. Sage Publications, Thousand Oaks, CA, 1995.
Westenholz, A.: From a Logic Perspective to a Paradox Perspective in the Analysis of an Employee Owned Company. *Economic and Industrial Democracy*, vol. 20, no. 4, pp. 503–534, 1999.
White, M.: *Narrative Practice and Exotic Lives: Resurrecting Diversity in Everyday Life*. Dulwich Centre Publications, Adelaide, 2004.

INDEX

Note: In this index, figures and tables are denoted by italic and bold text respectively. Text in text boxes is indicated by the suffix "b" after the page number.

Aarhus University 3, 26
acceptance, of complexity 53, **102**, 125, 144, 146–153, 157
action research 3, 26, 26–28
ambiguity: and ambivalence 104; and Birds-nest School 92; and communication 48, 51, 67b, 111–112, 147–148; in Lego 34, 118; and paradox 108, 150, 153b, 155, 156, 159; and persistent behavior 79; and sense-making model *32*; and transformation 31; and workable certainty 40–41
ambivalence: and ambiguity 104; and sense of belonging 100; and communication 106, 119; confronting one's own 119, 120b, 156; and control 101, 103, 119; in Lego 31, 34, 43, 101, 118, 147, 156, 161; and organizational change 101, 106, 113; and paradox 26, 101, 108, 109, 111, 112b, 118, 120b, 120, 156; and persistent behavior 79; and postmodern leadership 24; and trust 101, 103, 119; in Unimotor 116–117
asymmetrical manager–employee relationship 16
autonomy paradox 117–118

behavior: challenging 83–85; controlling 102; delegating 85–86; directive 14, 137; goal-driven 152; innovative employee 74; investigative 78–79; involving 86–89, 136; irrational 57, *58*; leadership 24, 138, 144–145; in Lego 31, 42; Management of Paradox Indicator 92; persistent 75, 79–80; positive opposite 135; practical 75, 76–77; role paradox 42; supportive 82–83; unconscious 57, *58*; visionary 75–76
Birds-nest School 91–92, 93, 96, 99
"blaming game" 147, 148
Blue Ocean strategy 74, 160

Carletti 61–67, 117
centralized-decentralized focus paradox 116
challenging-supportive paradox 82–85, 156
change *see* organizational change
change-stability paradox *see* stability-change paradox
coaching 15, 19–20, 21, 33, 82, 86, 123; Reinhard Stelter on 22
co-creation 55
commitment 14, 18, 21, 23, 24, 85; to welfare *54*, *63*, *66*
communication, organizational 40, 70, 118–119
competing values 53, 59, 60, 61, 68, 96, 132
competing paradigms *58*
Competing Values Framework (CVF) 53–58, *54*, *58*, 59, 61, 119, 157, 159
complex leadership 3–9
complexity: and acceptance of 157; and ambivalence 116, 119; and communication 67b, 120b, 147, 148;

Index

and Competing Values Framework 157;
  and integrative thinking 130; in Lego
  31, 34, 37, 42, 70; and organizational
  change 106; and paradox 109, 120b, 125,
  144, 155, 157, 159, 162; and paradoxical
  leadership 154, 162; and postmodern
  leadership 6, 9, 12, 43b, 146, 152; and
  reflective leadership 159; and sense of
  belonging 112; and sense-making model
  32; and workable certainty 40–41, 43,
  106, 156–157
complexity theory 150
conflict management *58*, 87
control-trust paradox 103, 106, 134, 141,
  142, 156
*Contradictions in Organization and Leadership
  Theory* 159
crisis, Chinese definition of 7
"cross-pressures" *see* paradoxes of belonging
CVF (Competing Values Framework) 53–58,
  54, *58*, 59, 61, 119, 157, 159

Danish Defense Academy 53–54
Danish elementary schools 70
decentralized-centralized focus
  paradox 116
defensive responses 38
delegating-involving paradox 85–87
Digmann, Anne Mette 72
dilemmas 10, 33, 42, 149
directing manager 16
double binds 111, 113, 116–117, 118, 119,
  120, *155*
"double loop-learning" 38
doubt 117, 136, 144–145, 155–156

emotional complexity 106
emotional exchange **21**
emotions 18, 39, 43, 100, 101, 103–104, 106
employee development 19, 62, 82, 134
employee-manager relationship 4, 16, 17,
  20, 21, *148*
empowerment 14, *54*, *63*, *66*, 108–109
exchange 16, 18, **21**

fear 64, 101, 103, 109, 137, *138*, 145, 158b
Fletcher's pendulum 140–141
Foucault, Michel 17, 20
functionalism **21**

Gittell, Jody 81
Goleman, Daniel 123–124, 159
"good leadership" 3, 9, 25, 89, 136, 138;
  Daniel Goleman on 124; in Lego 26,
  27; and organizational paradoxes 60,
  134, 161; "postmodern" paradigm 13; in
  Unimotor 116
Good to Great 108

Hamel, Gary 6
"hero-status" 5, 161
honesty-propriety paradox 118–119

indirect power 20, 22
individualism-team work paradox 156
individualization 19
influencing: employee 23, 87, 131;
  leadership as 15–16, 21
innovation, organizational 14
integrative thinking 123–131, 132, 140, 153,
  155, 157
intelligence, organizational 124, 125, 131,
  132, 145
investigative-persistent paradox 78–80
involvement 82, 86–87, *139*, 141, 148;
  in Carletti 65; employee 5, 27, 57, *58*;
  emotional 15, 18; in Lego 29, 69; role
  paradoxes **71**
involving-delegating paradox 85–87

Knudstorp, Jørgen Vig 108
Kotter, John 61
Kristiansen, Kjeld Kirk 26, 50–51

leadership: core task of 24; definitions of
  15–16, 21, 159; modern 16–17, 18, 20,
  96; as paradoxical task **21**, 22, 24, **25**, 25;
  postmodern 13, 14–15, 17–23, 23
leadership development 4, 54, 125, 134,
  138–139, 157
leadership paradigms: bridging the
  24–25, **25**, 96; modern *see* leadership,
  modern; postmodern *see* leadership,
  postmodern
leadership qualities 123, **135**
leadership roles 67, 69, 72–89, 99, 155;
  reflective 98b
leadership style 132, 133–134, 136–137,
  143, 144, 145; Birds-nest School
  96; bridging the paradigms 24, 96;
  coaching 123; Daniel Goleman on
  123–124; involved/ing 87, 132; in Lego
  27; pacesetting 123; postmodern 23;
  supportive 132; Unimotor 123
leadership theory 3–12, 107, 159
Leadership-based Coaching [book] 20
leadership-based coaching [concept]
  20, 59
Leading Change 61
Lego: A Company and its Soul 28

Lego: brainstorming process 31–33, *32*;
dilemmas 33, 42; eleven paradoxes of 27,
28–29, 43b; implementation center 31;
managerial issues 29–31; organizational
paradoxes in 47–50; paradoxes of
belonging in 101–104, **102**, **102**;
plumber metaphor 28; role paradoxes
in 69–72, **71**; workable certainty 31,
32, 40–43

Madsen, Benedicte 35
Management of Paradox Indicator
  (MPI) 11, 92
management team 8, 43b, 47, 59, 59b, 60,
  70, 84, 89b; mutual understanding within
  96–98; role clarification for 91–96, *93*,
  94; task clarification for 91–96
manager–employee relationship 4, 16, 17,
  20, 21, *148*
managerial flow 154–162
managerial reflection 42, 141
meeting forums *139*, 139
"mess" 32–35, *32*, 42
Mess and Cleanup in Organizations 35
modern leadership paradigm 16–17, 18, 20,
  21, 22, 24, **25**, 25, 96
modern power 20, **21**, 21, 22–23, 24
MPI (Management of Paradox
  Indicator) 11, 92
MUS (employee development
  interview) 19

openness 74, 78, 87
opportunities 7, 25b, 73, 101, 124, 158;
  employee potential 83; of paradoxes 161
optimism-realism paradox *see* Stockdale
  paradox
organizational change 5, 6, 48–50,
  61–67, *63*, *66*, 89, 119; acceptance, of
  complexity 125, 150; Birds-nest School
  99; Competing Values Framework 47, 72;
  emotional complexity 106–107; in Lego
  27, 40, 49; paradoxes 100–101; Linda
  Putnam on 70; taking responsibility for 78;
  Ralph Stacey on 150; Stockdale paradox
  108; Systemize 99; workable certainty 40
organizational communication 40, 70,
  118–119
organizational complexity 10, 116, 146,
  147, 154
organizational innovation 14
organizational intelligence 124, 125, 131,
  132, 145
organizational paradoxes 42, 47–60, **52**, *54*,
  63, *66*, *67*, 68–69, 72 *see also* Carletti;
centralized-decentralized focus paradox;
  change-stability paradox ; Competing
  Values Framework; Danish elementary
  schools; integrative thinking; Lego;
  results-relationships paradox
organizational relationships 56–57, 80–89,
  98, 99, 124, *155*
oscillation 133–134, 140, 142–144, 144b, 145

paradigms: bridging the 24–25, **25**, 96;
  competing *58*; modern leadership 16–17,
  18, 20, **21**, 22; postmodern leadership 13,
  14–15, 17–23, **21**, 22, 23
paradox, leadership through 158b
paradox exercise 134–137, **135**, *136*, *138*
paradoxes: emotional dimensions of
  109–110; external polarities of *63*;
  internal poles of *66*; interwoven
  155–157, *155*; leadership mindset 157
paradoxes of belonging 10, 43, 119–120b;
  autonomy paradox 117–118; connection
  with organizational and role paradoxes
  155, *155*; control-trust paradox
  113–117; emotional aspect 100–112,
  112b; honesty-propriety paradox 117–118;
  in Lego 43, **102**; propriety-honesty
  paradox 118–119; trust-control
  paradox113–117 *see also* Competing
  Values Framework; integrative thinking
Paradoxes of Group Life 103–104
paradoxical leadership 4, 13, 24–25,
  25, 143–144, 154, 157, 159 *see also*
  Birds-nest School
paradoxical perspective 9, 10, 104, 107, 159,
  160, 161–162
Paradoxical Thinking [book] 140
paradoxical thinking [concept] 26, 31,
  138, 161; acceptance of complexity
  148; Competing Values Framework
  88; leadership 89, 91, 119; in Lego 10;
  oscillation 133–134; in Vision Tech 127
paralysis: and ambivalence 116; meaning of
  9; of paradox 40, 150, 156, 157
persistent-investigative paradox 78–80
personal factors 133–134
personality tests 16, 133
Plougmann, Poul 26–27, 50–51
positioning *54*, *63*, *66*, 125, 132, 157
positioning theory 140–144, *142*
positive opposite 135–136, *136*
postmodern leadership paradigm 13, 14–15,
  17–23, **21**, 22, 23, 24, **25**, 25
power 17, 20, **21**, 21–22, 22–23, 24
practical-visionary paradox 75–77, 156
propriety-honesty paradox 118–119

public sector 8, 74, 160
"punctuation" 34
Putnam, Linda 70

rational exchange 16, 18, **21**
realism **21**, 74, 107
realism-optimism paradox 107–108
recognition, of paradox 8, 42, 126–127, 154
Red Ocean strategy 160
reflection 31, 33–34, 42, 157 *see also* Competing Values Framework; reflective distance
"reflective companion" 117
reflective distance 137–140; and competing values 132; and oscillation 140; relating to paradoxes 70–71, 125; and paradoxical leadership 144; and positioning 157
reflective leadership 33–34, 98, 139, 144, 154, 159
relationships: organizational 56–57, 80–89, 98, 99, 124, *155*; power **21**
relationships-results paradox 62, 85, 98, 119, 140, *155*, 156
Release the paradoxes! 158
result-oriented companies 55–56
result-oriented employees 80
results: competing paradigms *58*, 58; Competing Values Framework 54, *54*, 55–56; connection between paradoxes *155*; integrative thinking 123, 124; leadership roles 80–81; organizational change paradoxes 62, *63*, 64–65, *66*, 66; role paradoxes 73, *93*, 93, *94*, 98
results-relationships paradox 62, 85, 98, 119, 140, *155*, 156
role paradoxes 42, 89b, 158b; challenging-supportive paradox 82–85; Competing Values Framework 61; connections between paradoxes 155–157, *155*; delegating-involving paradox 85–87; investigative-persistent paradox 78–80; involving-delegating paradox 85–87; in Lego 69–72, **71**; persistent-investigative paradox 78–80; practical-visionary paradox 75–77; in practice 91–99, *93*, *94*; supportive-challenging paradox 82–85; visionary-practical paradox 75–77 *see also* Competing Values Framework; integrative thinking
role theory 140

satisfaction surveys 14, 19
sense-of-belonging paradoxes *see* paradoxes of belonging
sense-making *32*, *148*

"shared meaning" 7, 119
situational leadership 142–143
situation-based leadership model 86
SMART model 84b, 84
social capital 81
social intelligence 123, 124
social-constructionism 7, 15, 16, **21**, 21
Sørensen, Per 27–28, 28–29
stability 54, *54*, 57–58, *58*, *63*, *66*, 72–75, 77; employee need for 124; persistent behavior 79–80; role focus of leadership team *93*, 93, *94 see also* stability-change paradox
stability-change paradox 72, 74, 101, *155*, 156; Carletti 62, 63–64; Competing Values Framework 119, 140; Lego 49–50; Systemize 98; Vision Tech 127 *see also* stability
Stacey, Ralph 150, 159
Stockdale, Vice Admiral James Bond 107
Stockdale paradox 107–108
strategic development initiatives 63–67, *66*
strategic leadership action plan 119
supportive behavior 82–83
supportive-challenging paradox 82–85, 156
symmetry **21**, 21
Systemize 96–99

team work-individualism paradox 156
team-building 87
teamwork 14, 22, 53, *58*, 65, 83, 87, 91, 93, 154
The Future of Management 6
The Heart of Change 61
The Opposable Mind 125
Toyota 10
traditional power 17, **21**, 21
trust-control paradox 103, 106, 134, 141, 142, 156

Unimotor 113–117

Vision Tech 125–130
visionary-practical paradox 75–77, 156

Weick, Karl 7, 31–32, 34, 40
workable certainty 8, 12, 40–43, 106, 129, 152; paradoxes of belonging **102**, 108–109; definition of 6; integrative thinking 130; leadership 154, 156–157; in Lego 31; organizational paradoxes **52**, 148–149; oscillation 143; role paradoxes **71**; sense-making model *32*; in Unimotor 115 *see also* Competing Values Framework
"Working through Paradox" 10, 27, 31
workplace evaluation 19